STORIED &
SCANDALOUS
CHARLESTON

STORIED &
SCANDALOUS

CHARLESTON

A HISTORY OF **PIRACY** AND **PROHIBITION**, **REBELLION** AND **REVOLUTION**

LEIGH JONES HANDAL

Globe
Pequot

ESSEX, CONNECTICUT

Globe Pequot

An imprint of Globe Pequot, the trade division of
The Rowman & Littlefield Publishing Group, Inc.
4501 Forbes Blvd., Ste. 200
Lanham, MD 20706
www.rowman.com
Distributed by NATIONAL BOOK NETWORK

British Library Cataloguing in Publication Information available

Library of Congress Cataloging-in-Publication Data

Names: Handal, Leigh Jones, author.
Title: Storied and scandalous Charleston : a history of piracy and prohibition, rebellion and revolution / Leigh Jones Handal.
Other titles: Storied & scandalous Charleston
Description: Guilford, Connecticut : Globe Pequot, [2022] | Series: Storied & scandalous | Includes bibliographical references and index.
Identifiers: LCCN 2022007162 (print) | LCCN 2022007163 (ebook) | ISBN 9781493061853 (paperback ; alk. paper) | ISBN 9781493061860 (epub)
Subjects: LCSH: Scandals—South Carolina—Charleston—History. | Crime—South Carolina—Charleston—History. | Charleston (S.C.)—History—Anecdotes. | Charleston (S.C.)—Social life and customs—History.
Classification: LCC F279.C457 H37 2022 (print) | LCC F279.C457 (ebook) | DDC 975.7/915—dc23/eng/20220217

LC record available at https://lccn.loc.gov/2022007162
LC ebook record available at https://lccn.loc.gov/2022007163

∞™ The paper used in this publication meets the minimum requirements of American National Standard for Information Sciences—Permanence of Paper for Printed Library Materials, ANSI/NISO Z39.48-1992

CONTENTS

CONTENTS

CONTENTS

INTRODUCTION

Since Charleston's founding in 1670, never has a city better reflected the hedonistic nature of the man for whom it was named. When Charles II returned from exile to claim the English throne after more than a decade of dreary Puritan rule, he epitomized the image of a swashbuckling cavalier who ushered in the glorious era of the English Restoration with its bawdy theaters, witty playwrights, buxom mistresses, and first rate horse racing. Pennsylvania founder William Penn proclaimed colonial Charles Town "a hotbed of piracy," full of women "who frequented a tap room on The Bay and infected a goodly number of the militia with the pox." Decades later, Bostonian Josiah Quincy complained that Charlestonians "are devoted to debauchery and probably carry it to a greater length than any other people." And as the nineteenth century drew to a close, South Carolina governor Benjamin Tillman called Charlestonians "the most self-idolatrous people in the world." The reasons and culprits for such allegations can be found within these pages, as author Leigh Jones Handal dispels the myths of some old legends and recounts some lesser-known stories of Charleston's 350-year history of piracy, murder, eccentric characters, and the poignant, personal moments faced by those living on a daily basis with the realities of war, defeat, and numerous resurrections of their beloved city.

PART I
THE MERRY MONARCH
AND HIS HOLY CITY

s at least one Charleston historian has noted, perhaps no other city in America has ever been more aptly named than Charles Town,[1] so called for King Charles II, often referred to as the Merry Monarch, who in the mid-1600s ushered in the epoch known as the English Restoration. To understand Charleston, its people, and its history, one must first understand the nature and personality of Good King Charles himself, born at St. James's Palace on May 29, 1630, under the auspices of the planet Venus, goddess of love, beauty, pleasure, and wealth—all concepts central to the establishment of the Carolina colony that would bear his name. Thus Charleston's story must begin with a better understanding of England's Merry Monarch himself.

As a child, Charles enjoyed all the advantages of being England's heir apparent. By the time he was fourteen, however, the prince found himself in the battlefield alongside his father, fighting Puritan rebels in the English Civil War. As King Charles I realized his chances of victory were becoming

Charles II, born 1630, as Prince of Wales; painting ascribed to Justus Van Egmont (1601–1674). *WikiMedia Commons*

ever more elusive, he sought to protect his son and heir by sending him into exile at the court of his eight-year-old French cousin, King Louis XIV, where Charles's mother, Henrietta Maria, Louis XIV's aunt and the sister of King Louis XIII, had already taken refuge.

As he feared, by 1649 King Charles I had lost the war and was beheaded. The victorious Puritans, led by Oliver Cromwell, dismantled the monarchy and began transforming England into a rather somber place. The *Cambridge Dictionary* defines the word *puritan* as the belief that pleasure is wrong, an antonym of hedonism—or as early twentieth century author H. L. Mencken termed it: "the haunting fear that someone, somewhere, may be happy."[2] Upon their accession to power, these militant Calvinists outlawed most social and cultural pleasures, burning thousands of books feared to contain heretical ideas. They smashed classical works of art, tore down or boarded up theaters, outlawed horse racing and most other entertainments, kept the stocks and pillories filled with sinners of myriad transgressions, and even dictated the proper width and length of a lady's sleeves. (Heaven forbid, no lace allowed!)[3] Times were grim.

Charles II and the Lady Jane by Isaac Fuller (1606?–1672), showing Charles during his years as a young cavalier.
WikiMedia Commons

Meanwhile, the teenaged Charles II flourished in France, embracing French fashions, culture, and the company of the enticing ladies of the court. Here he grew into a "precocious maturity, cynical, self-indulgent, skilled in the sort of moral evasions that make life comfortable even in adversity."[4]

Even so, young Charles was only nominally supported through a small grant from his cousin Louis. As he grew older, Charles sought to advance his fortunes by traveling to other royal courts of Europe, seeking the support and charity of allied princes who might help finance his claim to regain his father's throne. Though Charles usually received warm receptions from his friends and relatives at these various courts, he unfortunately received virtually no tangible support for his cause. After nearly nine years traveling around France, Spain, and the Dutch Republic, Charles eventually ended up at The Hague as a guest of his sister Mary and her husband, William II, Prince of Orange.

During these travels, Charles established romantic liaisons with a number of women, both ennobled and obscure. While in The Hague in 1648, at the age of eighteen, Charles had a brief but quite public love affair with a Welshwoman of "middling gentry" named Lucy Walter, "of no good fame, but handsome," someone who "had not much wit" and a "great deal of that sort of cunning which those of her profession usually have."[5]

Lucy was the prince's first well-documented romantic liaison, though virtually all sources agree he had surely been sexually active from his early teens. Court rumors even suggested the couple had secretly married, though no reliable documentation of such an event has ever surfaced. Married or not, however, Charles openly recognized his paternity of their son, James Scott, who would eventually become the 1st Duke of Monmouth and 1st Duke of Buccleuch. Some historians have suggested that the marriage rumors were stoked when Charles declared his Catholic brother James II and VII heir to the throne, as it became increasingly apparent that Charles would have no legitimate children by his queen. Many would have preferred seeing Charles's first publicly acknowledged—though bastard—son, who was baptized a Protestant, taking precedence in the line of succession.

Without digressing too deeply into English history, suffice it to say that upon the death of Oliver Cromwell, there was a contested grab for power

Lucy Walter (1630–1658), artist unknown. *WikiMedia Commons*

among his protégés. Neither of the two principal contenders for the position was particularly well loved, and tensions were high. Fearing anarchy or another civil war, eight English gentlemen of wealth and influence (hereafter referred to as the True and Absolute Lords Proprietors of Carolina) feared that instability caused by the transfer of power could result in another civil war, an economic inconvenience that would likely, and adversely, affect their personal fortunes. To prevent that from happening, the eight noblemen pooled both their financial and influential resources and in 1660 successfully recalled Charles II from the continent to assume his father's former throne.

Upon his long-hoped-for accession, Charles II set about ushering in the period we know as England's Great Restoration Era: "the merry old England of bawdy theaters, wenches, witty playwrights, horse racing, formal gardens and easy virtue."[6] After more than a decade of pious Puritan rule, the English were ready for some excitement and vice, and Charles II was the man to bring it.

As his birth star had presaged, Charles had grown into a man who loved life, beauty, pleasures, and luxury, and he embraced them all with little reserve. Gone were the drab gray days of Puritan rule, and Charles quickly earned his popular nickname "The Merry Monarch" for the liveliness and hedonism of his court. Ladies could once again wear their sleeves in whatever style was fashionable at the moment with as much, or as little, lace as they pleased.

Charles was, of course, most grateful to the eight noblemen whose support and efforts on his behalf had restored him to the throne, and he needed to find a suitable means to express his appreciation. This he did by gifting them, ostensibly through his Divine Right as the King of England, with all the land in the New World south of Virginia, down to the Spanish colony of St. Augustine in Florida, and all the way west to the western coast, wherever that might lie. Of course the Spanish and French (not to mention the Native Americans who had lived here for millennia) had some doubts about Charles's Divine Right to present such a gift from a throne so far away across the sea, yet that is a discussion for another time. Charles felt the land was his to give, so he did.

The eight True and Absolute Lords Proprietors reconfirmed the colony's name of Carolina, a Latin feminine derivation originally meant to honor Charles I, and its capital, Charles Town (variously spelled Charles Towne, Charlestown, or Charlestowne), for Charles II. The spelling of the city's name throughout this text reflects what was most commonly used within the context of the time period being discussed, which prior to the American Revolution was Charles Town and afterward Charleston.

In nearly all aspects, early Charlestonians created their new colony based on the political and social customs of Charles's Restoration England. Perhaps most importantly, both economies were based principally on land ownership. The English political and economic system known as feudalism organized society within a formal, stratified structure that was dependent on one's ownership of real property, at the apex of which was a noble aristocracy who owned huge swaths of land known as baronies, duchies, or earldoms. Aside from a relatively small class of merchants, lawyers, clergymen, and artisans, pretty much everyone else toiled upon the noble lord's land for agricultural, mining, or forestry purposes as serfs, a population compensated with enough of life's necessities to survive, but not enough to advance their lots in life, and only very rarely that of their children. Thus the system perpetuated itself, passing down through generations the aristocracy's noble titles, land, and wealth through inheritance rather than through more egalitarian or meritorious means.

It doesn't take a great leap of imagination to see how that societal system readily transferred to the Carolina Lowcountry's plantation structure, now

King Charles II by John Michael Wright (1617–1694), c. 1661.
WikiMedia Commons

with the planter at the top of the hierarchy, a small class of artisans and merchants in the middle, and a huge enslaved labor force with only a miniscule chance of ever improving their lot in life. Charles Town was, in the very essence of its establishment, a small, re-created Restoration England.

At the risk of oversimplification, Charles II is generally remembered as a good king—or at least a tolerant one, if not a man of great genius, leadership, or political vision. One of his courtiers, John Wilmot, 2nd Earl of Rochester, summed up his sovereign with this verse:

> "We have a pretty, witty king,
> Whose word no man relies on
> He never said a foolish thing,
> And never did a wise one."[7]

True to his devil-may-care nature, Charles took the criticism in stride, acknowledging that there was some truth in the verse, as his words were indeed his own; however, he corrected, "my actions are those of my ministers."[8]

And so Charles embraced a diversity of scandalous pastimes within his court and his country, passions that were clearly reflected far across the Atlantic Ocean in the new colony that bore his name. What follows are just some of the ways in which Charleston has long reflected the hedonistic times and values of its revered namesake, King Charles II.

HOW CHARLESTON EARNED ITS NICKNAME "THE HOLY CITY"

A basically happy soul in most aspects, perhaps one of the most defining characteristics of Charles's nature to carry over into the psyche of Charles Town's settlers was that of religious tolerance. Though religion (Catholic, Anglican, or Dissenting) played a prominent role in English politics and society, Charles II never demonstrated himself to be a man of particularly strong personal convictions regarding his faith. Indeed, he seemed quite comfortable modifying his religious loyalties to suit political ends.

As an infant, Charles was baptized in the Church of England and reared by mostly Anglican guardians and mentors, though his French mother had been reared as a Catholic and his godparents, King Louis XIII and Marie de Medici, were devoutly so. Charles would show few enough qualms when, in 1670, he promised to adopt Louis XIV's Catholic faith in return for the French king's support in his war against the Dutch, though he never actually got around to confirming that conversion in any public ceremony. It was reported by some witnesses that Charles did finally convert to Catholicism on his deathbed, though some scholars suggest the "conversion" was staged by his Catholic brother and heir, James II and VII, after Charles lost consciousness.

Likewise, one of the most distinguishing features of Charles Town's founding was that, in contrast to many of its sister colonies in New England, there were no Puritans or Pilgrims here. The True and Absolute Lords Proprietors of Carolina had but one goal in mind as they began seeking settlers for their new colony, and that was what today we call "a return on their investment" for placing Charles II on the throne. Pamphlets distributed in Europe to encourage settlers depicted Charles Town as "a haven of religious toleration."[1] While Puritan settlers of the Massachusetts and Connecticut colonies were busy burning books and hanging witches, Charles Town's settlers maintained a laser-like focus on finding ways to make their financial fortunes in the New World. Capital gains, not spiritual concerns, was the name of the game in Charles Town.

John Locke, renowned English philosopher and close associate of one of the Lords Proprietors, Lord Anthony Ashley Cooper, Earl of Shaftesbury, clearly encouraged religious toleration as he drafted the Fundamental Constitutions of Carolina, the colony's first governing documents. Though the Fundamental Constitutions were never formally adopted as law in Carolina, in 1692 the colonial Assembly enacted legislation of its own extending the right to worship according to one's conscience[2]—with the exception of Catholics.

Catholics were ostracized during the colonial period, not on any theological basis but because of the fear that they somehow might be in league with their Spanish brethren in St. Augustine, who for many years continued to dispute Charles's prerogative to present the land between Virginia and St. Augustine to his noble cronies as a gift. To drive home their point, they would occasionally sail up the coast for a skirmish, and so were a thorn in the side of the early English settlers.

With that exception then, the Assembly's legislation allowed for even a handful of people who agreed on a theology to establish their own house of worship. Charles Town soon had so many churches, or "meetinghouses" as the Dissenters (Protestants other than Anglicans) called them, that the colony earned the moniker "The Holy City"—at least for its quantity of churches if not for the piousness of their congregations.

That is not to overlook the many important impacts made to early Charles Town by some religiously affiliated groups, such as the French Huguenots, who fled here and settled along the Santee River basin in 1685 after Louis XIV revoked the Edict of Nantes, which guaranteed French Protestants the right to worship as they chose. Yet these industrious Calvinists, who played a key role in establishing some of Carolina's earliest and largest plantations, were easily assimilated through marriage, language, and worship into Charles Town's culture, society, and Anglican congregations within a generation or two of their arrival.[3]

After the American Revolution, when Florida's Spanish settlers were no longer a threat, even Catholics found their place in Charleston. As early as 1801, the socially prominent Hibernian Society—a benevolent society established to assist Irish immigrants—alternated its annual presidency between a Catholic and a Protestant member. Perhaps nowhere else in eighteenth-century America could one find a Catholic church located directly across the street from the Jewish synagogue and around the block from the Protestant meetinghouse. Such toleration was unprecedented.

Indeed, Charleston has a long history as having one of the most robust Jewish communities in the New World, as Locke's Fundamental Constitutions specifically encouraged religious tolerance for "Jews, heathens, and dissenters." Charles Town's Jewish citizens could own land, serve in the militia, and run for office. Surviving voting records confirm that the Jewish community turned out in force to cast their ballots in the elections of 1702. By 1800, South Carolina had the largest Jewish population of any state in America.[4] Many were merchants; others became planters and military leaders.

Documentation from 1753 shows that while Muslims were few, they were not denied the right to practice their faith.[5] Quakers were welcomed through the end of the eighteenth century, when tensions began to escalate—again not over theological concerns but over the Friends' growing disapproval of slavery.[6] Baptists, Presbyterians, and Congregationalists all lived, worked, and prospered together in Charles Town.

Though the first ships to arrive in Charleston Harbor brought settlers of various (or even little) faiths, during the colony's first few decades the single strongest political faction to arrive comprised the scions of Barbadian sugar planters, who maintained strong ties to the king and his Anglican Church. Most often these were the second or third sons of West Indian plantation families, looking to make their own way in a world where the eldest son inherited everything. These settlers, many from wealthy families with good educations, sought to establish a society of "old-world elegance and frontier boisterousness. Ostentatious in their dress, dwellings and furnishings, they liked hunting, guns and dogs, military titles . . . [and] long hours at their favorite taverns over bowls of cold rum punch or brandy. In sum, the Barbadian well-to-do worked and played hard, drank and ate too much, spent recklessly, and often died young. . . . [T]hey sought the quickest routes to riches, and by 1674 they controlled both the Council and the popularly elected Assembly. . . . [They were] experienced, aggressive, ambitious, [and] sometimes unscrupulous."[7]

By 1706, this domineering group, commonly referred to as the Goose Creek Men, had pushed through laws establishing Anglicanism as the colony's established state religion. What that meant, however, had surprisingly little to do with how one worshipped. Known as the Church Act, it did more to create a political pathway for lay leaders of local Anglican parishes to attain governmental leadership positions. It also required that colonists pay taxes to the Church of England, which in Charles Town was in many ways a civic body as much as a religious one.

The Reverend Francis LeJau (also spelled Le Jau), sent into the Carolina wilderness as a missionary by the Society for the Propagation of the Gospel in Foreign Parts (SPGFP) in 1706, soon after the Church Act was passed, wrote to his sponsors in England that at first he thought the reason for the legislation's passage "was grounded upon true zeal for the glory of God," but was quickly disappointed to discern that it was actually for "revenge [and] self-interest."[8] Anglicanism remained South Carolina's state religion for the next seventy years, until after the American Revolution.

The need to recruit new settlers, then, goes a long way toward explaining why, as long as you worked hard and turned a profit, diverse religious views were so readily tolerated. Throughout the first century of Charles Town's existence, as long as one expressed a basic belief that God existed and dutifully paid one's taxes to the Anglican Church, one was free to worship according to one's conscience. Early Charlestonians, like King Charles himself, were much more interested in one's treasures here on Earth than those that may be laid away in Heaven.

THE GAYEST, WEALTHIEST PEOPLE IN AMERICA

The life of an early settler was never an easy one, despite the region's wealth of natural resources and a mostly supportive indigenous population. Therefore, the Lords Proprietors set about marketing the new colony in ways similar to how developers do it today, with the publication of brochures and advertisements touting the colony's straight, wide streets and claims that "the very air there gives a strong appetite and quick Digestion, that men find themselves . . . more lightsome . . . and that the Women are very Fruitful."[1]

Indeed, the settlers did make money, lots of it. As one of the five largest colonies in America before the American Revolution, Charleston supplied much of the world with exports of rice and indigo, reaping huge profits both in their cultivation and exportation. The collapse of Charleston's lucrative indigo industry after the American Revolution conveniently coincided with Eli Whitney's invention of the cotton gin in 1791, and cotton quickly filled the gap left by the post-Revolution cessation of indigo sales to England for the dyeing of military uniforms.

Conspicuous consumption, so enjoyed by Charles II himself, was the order of the day in colonial Charles Town, whether it was in the land-owners' great plantation mansions or urban town houses, their clothing, their luxurious imports, or their lavish entertainments. Bostonian Josiah Quincy, who, during his 1773 visit to Charles Town, relished in his many criticisms of its citizens, wrote to friends that "state, magnificence, and ostentation, the natural attendants of riches, are conspicuous among these people."[2] Quincy did include a favorable observation about one of his local hosts, however, as he recounted an elegant dinner party at the home of Miles Brewton, who Quincy described as "a gentleman of very large fortune": "the grandest hall I ever beheld, azure blue satin window curtains, rich blue paper with gilt, mashee borders, most elegant pictures, excessive grand and costly looking glasses. . . . At Mr. Brewton's sideboard was very magnificent plate: a very exquisitely wrought Goblet, most excellent workmanship and singularly beautiful. A very fine bird kept familiarly playing over the room, under our chairs and the table, picking up the crumbs, etc. and perching on the window, sideboard and chairs: vastly pretty."[3]

The Miles Brewton House, c. 1769, was visited by Bostonian Josiah Quincy during his 1773 visit to Charles Town. *WikiMedia Commons*

Other historical letter writers likewise found such dichotomies on which to comment during their visits to Charleston. Shortly after the American Revolution, French author and diplomat J. Hector St. John de Crèvecoeur wrote that Charlestonians "are the gayest in America; it is called the centre of our beau monde."[4] Later in the missive, however, de Crèvecoeur criticizes "the destruction that revolves around the slave-master relationships," making an appeal to a friend in the North that "slavery is a truly evil practice in the midst of the new nation of America."[5]

German physician and zoologist Dr. Johann B. Schoepf, upon his visit to Charleston in the late eighteenth century, wrote: "The people of Charleston live rapidly, not willingly letting go untasted any of the pleasures of life. . . . [L]uxury in Carolina has made the greatest advance, and their manner of life, dress, equipages, furniture, everything denotes a higher degree of taste and love of show, and less frugality than in the northern provinces."[6] How very reminiscent of Charles II.

THE SPORT OF KINGS

Among Charles II's many passions was the gentleman's sport of horse breeding and racing. As part of her wedding dowry, Charles's Portuguese queen, Catherine of Braganza (1638–1705), brought a number of mares to the royal stable, among them two named Bombay and Tangier, known as the "royal mares." Seventeenth-century English diarist and courtier of Charles II, Samuel Pepys, claimed their offspring were bred with Middle Eastern stallions to develop what we define today as Thoroughbreds.[1] Under Charles's rule, horse racing again became the sport of kings, a great revitalization after its abolishment by the Puritans.

That passion for horses was shared by those in Charles Town, where the races quickly became the center of the colony's entertainment and social life. Indeed, the racetrack established at the village of Childsbury, Carolina's first inland settlement, lasted long after the village itself had disappeared.[2] Charles Town's Newmarket Course (which shared its name with a popular racing venue in England) was hosting regular events years before the South Carolina Jockey Club, America's first horse-racing club, was established in 1758. With the opening of the Washington Race Course, named for the first US president following his 1791 visit to Charleston, February's annual Race Week became the central feature of Charleston's antebellum society scene for the next seven decades.[3]

In the 1773 letter describing his visit to Charles Town, Josiah Quincy noted that "Cards, dice, the bottle and horses engross the prodigious portions of time and attention; the gentlemen (planters and merchants) are mostly men of turf and gamesters."[4]

16

Cockfighting was a popular side diversion at Charles Town's horse races—hardly surprising, as Charles II and his fellows likewise enjoyed the bloody sport. Indeed, John Locke and his patron, Lord Proprietor Anthony Ashley Cooper, drew up their "Grande Modell of Charles Town," laying out the new colony's streets and public spaces while drinking and betting in a cockfighting gallery, where they watched the enraged fouls rip each other to shreds with spurs attached to their flailing feet. Today the historic popularity of the sport is recalled in the state university's athletic mascot, the University of South Carolina's Fighting Gamecocks. Unfortunately, the inhumane blood sport is still illegally practiced throughout the state today on a far-too-frequent basis.

TRIPPING THE LIGHT
FANTASTIC

Charles II was a generous patron of the arts. In addition to supporting the work of poets, writers, musicians, and fine artists, he reopened and rebuilt many of the theaters destroyed by Cromwell's Puritans. Under Charles's patronage, bawdy Restoration comedies, the late seventeenth- and early eighteenth-century satires of manners, became popular, encouraging the use of sexually provocative language and innuendos. In addition, Charles insisted that theatrical companies begin casting women in female roles rather than have those parts played by slightly built young men, as had long been customary.

From the early years of the eighteenth century, Charlestonians also were treated to a regular fare of theatrical performances in various locales around the city, as before 1736 plays and concerts were most often held in the long rooms of local taverns. As early as 1702, Anthony Ashton, a traveling English actor, wrote of returning home from his military service with Carolina's Proprietary Governor James Moore in an attack on St. Augustine: "We arrived in Charles Town full of lice, shame, poverty, nakedness and hunger. . . . I turned player and poet, and wrote one play on the subject of the Country."[1] This performance is considered by many to be the first professional theatrical performance in North America.

On February 8, 1735, Charles's namesake city also became the first to stage a documented operatic performance in America. Held in the long room of Shepherd's Tavern at the corner of Broad and Church Streets, *Flora, or Hob in the Well*, was among the first theatrical shows to combine contemporary music with lyrics to create opera. The performance was well received, so much so that it inspired Charlestonians to undertake the construction of a public theater.

"The new theatre in Dock Street" opened February 12, 1736, with a comedy titled *The Recruiting Officer*, according to an advertisement in the *South-Carolina Gazette*.[2] This documentation makes it one of the oldest buildings, if not the first, built specifically for theatrical performances in America. The theater's original entrance faced north onto what was officially named Queen Street, but more commonly called at the time Dock Street because of the wharf on its eastern terminus. Sometime after Queen Anne's ascension in 1702, the Lords Proprietors renamed the thoroughfare Queen Street in her honor. In those days, however, word traveled slowly across the vast Atlantic Ocean, and even then, old habits were hard to break. It took a number of years for locals to catch on to the new name.

That theater, whose name was documented only that one time in the *Gazette* advertisement, was short-lived. Though no accounts of its demise survive, it may have burned down four years after its opening in the Great Fire of 1740. Subsequent ads in the *South Carolina-Gazette* indicate that a new theater had opened at the same location by 1754, and its seasonal runs for 1763–1766 were published in the newspaper. By the time of the American Revolution, however, this theater, too, had inexplicably disappeared from the historical record.

Yet Charleston continued to honor Charles II's legacy as a patron of the theater and musical performances when, in 1935, DuBose Heyward, working with his wife, Dorothy, and the Gershwin brothers, Ira and George, composed America's first native opera, *Porgy and Bess*—a poignant story of love, loss, and betrayal among Charleston's downtrodden urban African-American neighborhoods in the early part of the twentieth century. Even today, Charles II's love of theater and the arts lives on in Charleston through the city's annual spring Spoleto Festival. Surely, were he alive, Charles II would be among Spoleto's biggest patrons.

A LEGACY OF
ILLICIT LOVE

Another characteristic historically associated with port cities such as
Charleston is a thriving industry in the world's oldest profession. That
legacy of illicit love has permeated Charleston's history as yet another of King
Charles II's hedonistic influences, one that continued well into the twentieth
century, as Charleston's devastated post–Civil War economy finally began to
revive itself thanks to the installation of a US naval base and shipyard along
the banks of the Cooper River, just north of the city's downtown center.

In her doctoral dissertation, Krystle Kline writes:

> At the turn of the century, moral reformers in America targeted
> prostitution as the "Great Social Evil." Some portrayed prostitutes
> as sympathetic young victims of white slavery, while others viewed
> them as diseased bodies that infected America's soldiers and young
> men. In Charleston, S.C., however, the middle and upper classes
> voiced little concern over the city's red light district, which was
> located near the central business district. When the federal gov-
> ernment launched a nationwide investigation into forced prostitu-
> tion in 1912, they sent agents to Charleston. Although the federal
> agents made their findings public, Charlestonians made no effective
> efforts to reform or shut down the vice district. The local citizenry,
> police and politicians quietly tolerated prostitution while police col-
> lected fines from madams in the vice district. Most of Charleston's

prostitutes fit the typical profile of American prostitution, young women far from home who became a prostitutes for economic reasons. Without much oversight, some madams gained a large degree of autonomy and control over their own lives. In 1918 the federal government closed Charleston's vice district, and prostitutes' lives became materially worse. Madams shut down their brothels, and prostitutes began to work on the streets. A 1920 federal public health investigation reveals prostitutes' increased dependence on pimps and male taxicab drivers, and prostitution began to emerge in its modern form.[1]

Like the prodigious use of alcohol, prostitution and the keeping of mistresses in Charleston goes back to its earliest days. Documentation from 1702 notes that women of "ill fame" openly approached men on the streets in the evening hours.[2] In 1703, the Colonial Assembly passed legislation preventing "Mens Cohabitating with women with whom they are not married, & against Strumpets" and in September of that same year passed an Act Against Bastardy.[3] Still, little changed.

Charles Town's colonial act against bastardy brings with it an especially rich irony when drawing parallels between the social values of the young colony and the character of its namesake. For if there was anything Charles II loved more than the arts, good food and wine, horse racing, and dog breeding, it was women. As in the case of Charles's affair with Lucy Walter and their son, James Scott, bastardy readily came along with the king's many love affairs.

Despite his philandering nature, evidence suggests that Charles loved— or at least fondly cared for—his wife, Queen Catherine of Braganza. Years before the young prince's exile to France, negotiations had begun between the English and Portuguese courts for the children's betrothal. Despite the fact that Charles had been romantically linked to numerous women during his exile and travels to various European courts, marital negotiations with Portugal were quickly revived and completed upon his ascension to the throne in 1660.

Queen Catarina de Bragança (1638–1705) by Peter Lely, 1665. *WikiMedia Commons*

Charles and Catherine were married in May 1662. The bride brought with her a very attractive dowry, including not only the fine horses aforementioned but also the North African country of Tangier, the Seven Islands of Bombay, trading privileges with Brazil and the East Indies, and two million Portuguese crowns. In return, Charles promised England's support in Portugal's fight for independence from Spain and agreed that Catherine would be free to remain a Catholic if she chose.[4] No surprise there, given Charles's tendency toward religious tolerance.

A year after their nuptials, Catherine suffered one of three documented miscarriages. Afterward, she was ill for quite some time and became delirious enough to imagine she had successfully given birth, a fiction Charles supported and ordered her attendants to support until she was well enough to know the truth. Throughout their marriage, Charles insisted that Catherine be treated with the respect due her as both his wife and a queen in her own right. Catherine's story creates an interesting contrast with that of Henry XIII's first wife, Catherine of Aragon. As with Henry and Catherine, many of Charles's advisers urged him to divorce Catherine after several miscarriages left him without a legitimate heir. Yet Charles refused to do so time and again, asserting her rightful position as his queen consort.

By all accounts, Catherine remained faithful to Charles throughout their marriage, despite the humiliation she must have endured on account of his openly adulterous relationships. On his deathbed in 1685, Charles asked for Catherine to come to him, but she declined, asking him to excuse her absence and forgive her if she had ever offended him. Charles responded to her messenger: "Alas, poor woman! she asks for my pardon? I beg hers with all my heart, take her back that answer."[5]

Yet marriage did nothing to curb Charles's voracious love life, one which he had cultivated well before his marriage and which he vigorously maintained thereafter. Though exactly how many women Charles had affairs with will undoubtedly forever remain an unsubstantiated footnote in history, documentation exists for at least a dozen significant, publicly acknowledged liaisons. And though Queen Catherine never gave Charles any legitimate heirs, male or female, the lusty king publicly acknowledged and supported at least twelve children born to seven of his mistresses.

As always, Charles was quite open-minded and tolerant in affairs of the heart. He seduced both Catholics and Protestants with equal fervor, women of wealth from great families as well as those of low birth. He seemed to have a particular fondness for actresses (at least four of his liaisons trod the theatrical boards) and ladies with a bit of girth on them. (Who among us over forty can't appreciate that?) Perhaps to his credit, Charles also had an appreciation for smart, witty women with a good sense of humor, even more so than traditional aristocratic beauties, though he often availed himself of the latter's charms as well.

Perhaps the most politically powerful, though unpopular, of Charles's mistresses was Barbara (née Villiers) Palmer—a tall, voluptuous woman with whom he acknowledged fathering at least five of her six children (though according to Barbara, her youngest daughter was also Charles's; Charles had his doubts). Barbara's father, William Villiers, had supported Charles I in the English Civil War, spending most of the family's fortune on horses, ammunition, and other military supplies before being killed in the Battle of Bristol, leaving Barbara and her mother in dire straits financially. Lady Villiers resolved this set-back by marrying her first husband's cousin, Charles Villiers, 2nd Earl of Anglesey.

While under Puritan rule, the Villiers family maintained a surreptitious loyalty to the exiled Prince Charles. Each year on the prince's May 29 birthday, they would quietly gather in their wine cellar and toast to Charles's health and return.[6] Surely such devotion contributed to Barbara's fascination with the prince who would one day become her paramour.

At the age of nineteen, Barbara married Roger Palmer, a Catholic whose family disapproved of the union and predicted that Barbara would make their son "one of the most miserable men in the world."[7] Indeed, within the first year of the Palmers' marriage, Barbara began her longtime affair with Charles, soon after his 1660 return to England and two years before his marriage to Queen Catherine.

Yet here again, Charles's licentious behavior is balanced by a more amiable side of his nature: In return for Barbara's affections, Charles ennobled her husband, Roger Palmer, as Baron Limerick, 1st Earl of Castlemaine. Barbara herself was titled Duchess of Cleveland in her own right. Yet before the pendulum swings too far in Charles's favor, it's worth noting that the Palmers' advancements were predicated on the condition that only Barbara's children (who were also Charles's, not Palmer's) would inherit these noble titles and properties rather than any issue Palmer produced, either with Barbara or someone else. The Palmers' titles would pass only to Charles's children.[8] In this way then, Charles took responsibility and provided for his and Barbara's illegitimate offspring, one of whom was born each year from 1661 to 1664:[9]

- Lady Anne Palmer Fitzroy (b. 1661), whose paternity was claimed by both Charles and Roger Palmer, as well as by one of Barbara's other lovers at the time, the Earl of Chesterfield. Because Charles's claim took precedence over the other two, Anne later assumed the title "Fitzroy," meaning "child of the King," as would her siblings. Upon her marriage she became the Countess of Sussex.
- Charles Palmer Fitzroy (b. 1662) was also claimed by both Charles and Palmer and later assumed the surname Fitzroy like his older sister. Palmer originally christened Charles in the Catholic faith, but several days later King Charles had him rechristened in the Anglican Church. Following baby Charles's birth, Barbara and Roger Palmer

separated, though never divorced. Charles Fitzroy was ennobled as Lord Limerick, 1st Duke of Southampton and 2nd Duke of Cleveland, thus inheriting the title Charles had bestowed upon Barbara. He leaves behind a scandalous legacy of his own: Upon the death of his betrothed wife's father, he abducted his wealthy eight-year-old bride-to-be from her guardians with the intention of rearing her along with any children he could father upon her. Pretty sick when you think about it.

- Henry Fitzroy (b. 1663) never used the surname Palmer following the breakup of his mother's marriage. Charles II named him Earl of Euston and Duke of Grafton. Henry went on to achieve a respectable military career before he was killed in battle when he was twenty-seven.
- Charlotte Fitzroy (b.1664) married Edward Lee, 1st Earl of Lichfield, at the age of thirteen and thus became the Countess of Lichfield. The couple had at least eighteen offspring who survived childhood. (And, as we truly do say in Charleston, "Bless her heart!")
- George Fitzroy (b. 1665) was ennobled as the Earl of Northumberland and Duke of Northumberland. Shortly after his marriage, he and his brother Henry secretly abducted his new wife and hid her away in an unidentified nunnery. The couple (obviously) had no children.
- Barbara Fitzroy (b. 1672) was probably fathered by John Churchill, Duke of Marlborough, though Barbara claimed the girl to be Charles's. In this case, however, the king denied paternity. Little Barbara, with no titles and little hope for a good marriage, became a nun.

Contemporaries wrote with disparate opinions of Barbara Villiers Palmer's character, some considering her to be "great fun, keeping a good table and with a heart to match her famous temper."[10] Perhaps more telling, however, was her contentious relationship and struggle for power with Queen Catherine. The royals married shortly before the birth of Barbara's and Charles's second child, Charles Palmer Fitzroy, and while the newlyweds

Barbara Palmer, 1st Duchess of Cleveland, by Henry
Gascar (1635–1701). *WikiMedia Commons*

were away on their honeymoon, Barbara brazenly moved into Catherine's
rooms at Hampton Park Palace to have her baby.

Despite Catherine's shock, Charles continued his affair with Barbara openly, to the point where many referred to her as "The Uncrowned
Queen." To add insult to injury, Charles then elevated Barbara to the position of Lady of the Queen's Bedchamber, despite Catherine's objections. Stories of the ladies' heated confrontations behind closed doors kept the court
entertained for years, eventually culminating in what became known as the
"Bedchamber Crisis." Charles settled the matter apparently in Barbara's
favor, sending Catherine's personal retinue of ladies in waiting, her inner
circle of friends, back to Portugal. As a result, Catherine came to understand
that her lot in life was to accept Charles's mistresses as having a recognized,
if not official, status at court.

Yet Charles was no more faithful to Barbara than he was to Catherine, and his interests soon moved elsewhere, at which point he bestowed upon Barbara several new properties and titles, something he often did before breaking off an affair, as if to assuage his conscience. Meanwhile, Barbara had converted to her husband's Catholic faith, perhaps to spite Charles. It wasn't her most strategic move, however, as within a year of her giving birth to her last daughter, Parliament passed the Test Act, which banned Catholics from holding public office. Thus her conversion gave Charles cause to dismiss Barbara from her position as Lady of the Bedchamber (no doubt to Queen Catherine's great relief), after which he advised her to "live quietly and cause no scandal as he 'cared not whom she loved.'"[11]

Barbara set out for Paris, where she continued to live lavishly and love often, going heavily into debt thanks to a fondness she developed for gambling. Nevertheless, and true to his tolerant nature, years later, less than a week before his death, Charles was seen enjoying one last merry late dinner with Barbara, undoubtedly reminiscing about old times.

Eleanor "Nell or Nellie" Gwyn (sometimes spelled Gwynn or Gwynne) was everything Barbara Villiers Palmer was not. Indeed, perhaps she, as much as Charles himself, embodied the raucous spirit of the English Restoration that was to permeate Charles Town's settlement. One of the first actresses to take the stage upon Charles's decree to cast women in their

Portrait of Nell Gwyn (1650–1687), mistress of Charles II of England, by Simon Pietersz Verelst (1644–1721). In this image, Nell holds a jasmine, a reference that artists of that time included to indicate the amiable nature of their subject. *WikiMedia Commons*

rightful roles, Nell quickly cultivated a reputation as the Lucille Ball of her day, with one critic referring to her as "pretty, witty Nell."[12]

Though there is more folklore than reliable documentation about Nell's life, it seems that for the most part, hers was probably a classic rags-to-riches Cinderella story. Oral traditions claim that Nell's mother, who ran a tavern (or maybe even a brothel, depending upon the storyteller), drowned after falling down drunk into a ditch. Stories about Nell's father include one that claims he was born into a respected old Welsh family, while others say he was a ne'er-do-well who died in prison.[13] Regardless, it seems that Nell was likely reared by a single mother who had to make a living the best way she could for herself and her children. Some sources go so far as to claim that Nell was a child prostitute, although no reliable documentation supports this. At any rate, it's a good bet that Nell grew up fast and resilient, with plenty of street smarts.

According to oral tradition, Charles and Nell met at a theater, where apparently Charles paid more attention to Nell than to the play, and after which he invited her to dine with him, his brother, James, and several others at a nearby tavern. According to the story Nell herself told, Charles and James both suddenly "discovered" that they had no money on them to pay for the meal, leaving her to pick up the tab—to which she responded good-naturedly that "this is the poorest company I ever was in!"[14] It has been said that Nell, who also had affairs with fellow actor Charles Hart and Charles Sackville, 6th Earl of Dorset, referred to her lovers as Charles I, II, and III.

Nell gave Charles two acknowledged sons. Folklore holds that when the elder son, Charles (b. 1670), was six years old, Nell called him saying, "Come here, you little bastard, and say hello to your father." The king admonished Nell for her use of the derogatory term, to which she replied that she had no other name by which to call him. Charles parried the retort by giving him the last name of Beauclerk and naming him the Earl of Burford, as well as the 1st Duke of St. Albans. The couple's second son, James Beauclerk, was born just a year after his brother and died at the age of ten while studying abroad in France.

Throughout their many years together, Charles kept Nell close by, providing her with a brick town house at 79 Pall Mall, where she lived for the rest of her life.[15] Here, Nell enjoyed entertaining her many friends, including a few of Charles's other mistresses with whom she was friendly and her own lovers as well, whom she continued to acquire throughout her long relationship with the king.

Though often portrayed as a bit scatterbrained, Nell was known for her quick wit and humor, including an incident recounted in the memoirs of the Comte de Gramont: "Nell Gwynn was one day passing through the streets of Oxford, in her coach, when the mob mistaking her for her [Catholic] rival, the Duchess of Portsmouth, commenced hooting and loading her with every opprobrious epithet. Putting her head out of the coach window, 'Good people', she said, smiling, 'you are mistaken; I am the Protestant whore.'"[16]

As with Queen Catherine, Charles fondly remembered Nell on his deathbed in 1685, admonishing his brother, James, to "Let not poor Nelly starve." James honored his brother's request, paying off Nell's debts and granting her an annual pension of £1,500 for life. He also paid the outstanding mortgage on Nell's country property, Nottinghamshire Lodge, which remained in her family until 1940.[17] Nellie herself died just three years after Charles, allegedly of syphilis.

The "Catholic whore" to whom Nell referred in the incident recounted above by the Comte de Gramont was Louise Renée de Penancoët de Kéroualle, the French aristocratic Duchess of Portsmouth. Nellie Gywn and Louise differed in nearly every aspect, and were both rivals and friends in turn. The two often took afternoon tea together and enjoyed playing cards.[18]

By the time Louise came to the English court to serve as Queen Catherine's new lady-in-waiting following the dismissal of Barbara Palmer, she had already established a long history with Charles and his family. In addition to being King Louis XIV's sister-in-law during the time of Charles's exile there, Louise had also served as a lady-in-waiting to Charles's sister, Henrietta. Henrietta's sudden death in 1670 while visiting her brother left Louise at loose ends, prompting Charles to appoint her to the queen's retinue. Unlike Barbara Palmer, however, Louise showed Queen Catherine her due respect and loyalty, and the two forged a friendship despite their "shared interest" in Charles.[19]

Still, Louise was quite unpopular with most of Charles's subjects, per-haps because of her Catholic faith, though another factor surely could be attributed to rumors that Louise was a spy for the French court. While there is some evidence for that claim, including lavish gifts and monetary pensions from King Louis XIV, who gave her a pair of earrings reportedly worth £18,000, far more than any gift the French court had ever extended to Queen Catherine, most scholars consider the innuendos inconclusive.[20] Other sources suggest her promiscuity contributed to her unpopularity, though that seems odd given the promiscuousness of Charles's other mis-tresses, including both Barbara Palmer and Nellie Gwyn.

Nevertheless, Louise "concealed a great cleverness and a strong will under an appearance of languor and had a childlike beauty, yielded only when she had already established a strong hold on Charles's affections and character."[21] Her royal bastard, yet another named Charles, was born in 1675 and ennobled as the 1st Duke of Richmond.

Louise Renée de Penancoët de Kéroualle (1649–1734) by Peter Lely (1618–1680). *WikiMedia Commons*

As with Nell, Charles loved Louise for the rest of his life. He even named a royal yacht the HMY *Fubbs,* "Fubbs" being an affectionate nickname he gave Louise for her chubbiness.[22] As with Queen Catherine and Nellie Gwynn, upon his deathbed, Charles asked his brother, James, to "do well by Portsmith." Unlike Nell, however, James did not support Louise, and she returned to France, where she died in 1734.

Charles had many other mistresses, including Moll Davis, Elizabeth Killigrew, and Catherine Pegge, all of whom gave Charles acknowledged children. Undoubtedly there were many other lovers and many other bastards, though he chose to only acknowledge twelve. His virility earned Charles yet another nickname, "Old Rowley," in honor of his favorite racehorse, who was a notable stallion.[23]

An interesting footnote before moving on from the impact of King Charles II on the founding of Charleston: As previously noted, Charles fathered no legitimate children to inherit his throne, which passed instead to his brother. Nevertheless, within our lifetime, the first direct descendant of the Merry Monarch may finally assume the British throne, and when he does, it will not be through the genes of either Queen Elizabeth II nor her son Prince Charles. Lady Diana Spencer, mother of Princes William and Harry, is a direct descendant of both Henry Fitzroy, 1st Duke of Grafton and Charles's son with Barbara Palmer, and Charles Lennox, 1st Duke of Richmond and Charles's son with Louise de Kéroualle. Assuming Prince William will one day sit upon the British throne, he will become the first direct descendent of Charles II to do so. Clearly, Charles II's legacy continues to thrive in England, as it has through the history of the American city that bears his name.

PART II
DANCE OF THE
HEMPEN JIG

CHARLES TOWN'S PIRATICAL HEYDAY

Pirates weren't always the bad guys—at least not if you asked merchants along East Bay and Elliott Streets during Charles Town's piratical heyday. From its founding in 1670 through the first two decades of the eighteenth century, Charles Town was a favorite port for privateers looking to sell stolen goods at reasonable prices.

Privateering, that is the looting of foreign ships during times of war, was legal—indeed patriotic—as long as one obtained a governmentally issued license.[1] And in those days, when wasn't there a war going on among the various European countries fighting for possession of the New World? The War of Spanish Succession (1702–1713), known in Charles Town as Queen Anne's War, was one such conflict fought among the British, Spanish, and French over disputed rights to colonial territories. It was common practice for each nation to issue its warships licenses to attack and plunder enemy ships: "our" good guys attacking "their" bad guys, with legitimacy, of course, depending on which side you were on.[2]

Despite typical settlement hardships and recurring epidemics, Charles Town was thriving as the eighteenth century dawned. Barbadian traders were pushing the edge of the colony's frontier ever farther inland along the western branch of the Cooper River, and the French Huguenots who had arrived a decade or so earlier were developing burgeoning rice and indigo operations along the Cooper's eastern branch as well as in the Santee River basin, establishing the foundation on which South Carolina's storied plantation society would be built. Conveniently situated as Charles Town was at the western terminus of the great Atlantic coastal highway, the colony's harbor was filled with ships and robust economic opportunities.

Within this context, privateers arrived in Charles Town flush with purses full of "hard money"—gold and silver coins—and they spent lavishly on food, drink, supplies, accommodations, entertainment, and other goods while in port. In addition, Charlestonians relied on the privateers, "private men of war [with] letters of marque from Great Britain,"[3] to help protect the colony against French and Spanish marauders.

Admittedly the seamen could be a rowdy bunch, more often than not prone to fighting, damaging property, intimidating locals, and leering at

The Alexander Peronneau House, a double tenement at 141–145 Church Street, is touted by many as a former bordello where pirates found room and board while in town. Some claim a tunnel below it provided an escape route to the colony's wharves, though no tunnel has ever been found—and digging tunnels in a city as low-lying as Charleston provides challenges in and of itself. Despite the picturesque anchor that adorns the front of the house today, it is unlikely that pirates ever stayed at this residence, which was built in 1740, long after pirates had disappeared from Charles Town. However, they may have frequented an earlier structure at this location, which would have been close to the city's eighteenth-century market. *Library of Congress*

respectable young women. Though good for the local economy, they also brought trouble, a general concern or uneasiness, along with them while in port. The privateers' disruption of sanctioned (that is, lawfully taxed) trade was an ongoing concern for the Lords Proprietors, and as early as 1684, England's Privy Council passed an act mandating that Charles Town merchants suppress any and all illegal maritime trade.

Yet not much changed as a result of the act. Local officials were hesitant to arrest the privateers, and thereby interfere with their impact on the local economy, nor were they motivated to investigate the legality of the mariners' supply chain. One Charles Town merchant reacted to the Privy Council's act by complaining that those who cracked down on pirates were "Enemys of the Countrey."[4] For the most part, customs officials were quite willing to accept bribes in return for allowing Charles Town's merchants and privateers to continue doing business as usual. And so, despite the Privy Council's edict, Charlestonians continued to trade with these "cutthroats [who] were also cut-rate traders, and London wasn't sending them any cheaper supplies."[5] But that perspective was about to change.

The Peace of Utrecht, reached in 1713, brought an end to Queen Anne's War, and with it the end of government-sanctioned privateers' licenses. The marauders of the sea suddenly found themselves out of a job, one which they had enjoyed and profited from immensely. Many, if not most, were unwilling to settle for more mundane, lower-paying occupations back on land, and so they continued their pillaging industry by raiding any ship they came across, regardless of which nation's flag it flew. Formerly legal privateers now became full-fledged pirates, seafaring thieves who ruthlessly plundered, kidnapped, killed, and raped at will, operating entirely outside of any country's law.

Pirate attacks reached their peak along the Carolina coast in the late 1710s, when captains such as Edward Teach (aka Blackbeard), Stede Bonnet, Richard Worley, and Charles Vane began sacking local ships carrying rice, indigo, animal pelts, and other trade goods between Charles Town and European markets. Now, not only were the buccaneers interrupting commerce, they had also begun to threaten lives and undermine the economic and political stability of the colony.[6] Once Charlestonians became the victims, rather than the beneficiaries, of the pirates' looting, public support for them quickly reversed itself. By 1716, Charlestonians, even the merchants, had had it with these guys.

In 1716 the colony was recovering from a victorious but devastating war with the native Yamasee tribes the previous year.[7] Politically powerful Barbadian traders, known as the Goose Creek Men, beseeched the colony's Lords Proprietors to send help and supplies to defeat the Yamasee, but their pleas fell on deaf ears. The Proprietors responded to colonists' requests for help by reminding them that they had warned them, without effect, that selling Native Americans to Caribbean slave traders was bound to end badly at some point. Nor would the Proprietors step in now and rescue the colony from the pirates, this time reminding them of their contempt for the Privy Council's act of 1684, banning Charlestonians from doing business with the privateers. On both counts, the Lords Proprietors said, the colonists had made their own bed and should now not be surprised to have to sleep in it.

Proprietary Governor Robert Johnson stepped up to the challenge when a group of pirates marooned off Charles Town's coast came into town one day seeking help from their old merchant friends.[8] To their surprise, Governor Johnson had them quickly rounded up and hanged within sight of ships moored in the harbor—a clear message that pirates were no longer welcome in Charles Town. The South Carolina Commons House of Assembly then passed a resolution prevailing upon Capt. Thomas Howard, commander of the HMS *Shoreham*, to defend the colony against the "pirates of the Bahamas."[9] By 1718, Col. William Rhett, an officer of the provincial militia, receiver-general of Carolina, surveyor, controller of customs, and a sea merchant himself, refitted two of his ships, the *Henry* and the *Sea Nymph,* with eight guns each and a crew of sixty to seventy men to hunt down any pirates who were terrorizing the Carolina coast.

By the fall of 1718, at least fifty-eight buccaneers had been captured, charged with piracy, and tried before Judge Nicholas Trott in the South Carolina Court of Vice Admiralty. Judiciary records detailing their trials show that within the course of thirteen trials spread over five weeks, only nine defendants were determined to be not guilty and their lives spared.[10]

The others were all ordered to "dance the hempen jig," a euphemism for hanging until dead along Charles Town's waterfront, their bodies clearly visible to ships anchored in the harbor. Some corpses, usually those of captains or ringleaders, were left hanging for days to rot in the sun as a warning to anyone who might be thinking of taking up the pirate's vocation. Others were hung in chains or displayed in mounted cages, to the same effect.[11]

Many were executed at the site of what is today the city's popularly picturesque White Point Gardens. Legend, though no hard evidence, holds that many who were hanged from White Point's stately oak trees were buried in the shoreline's pluff mud below the high-tide mark (as burying even executed criminals was still the good Christian thing to do). The incoming tide would naturally unearth the bodies through no fault of the dutiful churchmen who "buried" them, the bodies washing in and out with the currents for days before sinking to their final resting place in the muck of the harbor's bottom, leaving only their legends behind.

Most of those legends, and what we think we know today of the pirate's life, comes to us through a handful of seasoned storytellers such as Capt. Charles Johnson, who in 1724 wrote *A General History of the Robberies and Murders of the most notorious Pyrates*. Many scholars have suggested that Captain Johnson was a nom de plume for Daniel Defoe, author of *Robinson Crusoe*, published in 1719 and so popular that some credit it as being second only to the Bible in its number of translations.[12] Others suggest the captain's true identity to be Nathaniel Mist, an early eighteenth-century London newspaper publisher who regularly wrote articles about the great Atlantic pirates of the New World.

Regardless of the author's true identity, these dramatically enhanced stories have shaped the way we remember pirates today, down to their eye patches, wooden peg legs, and smart-mouthed parrots. Though the tales are woefully short on documentation, the legends have been passed down as history for generations. In a subsequent edition of *Pyrates*, Captain Johnson defended accusations concerning his lack of sources by noting that if the reader found the book to be entertaining, "we hope it will not be imputed as a Fault, but as to its Credit."[13] Thus he and other great eighteenth-century storytellers have shaped the world's imaginations of life on the high seas for more than three centuries. Still the old adage holds true: The truth can sometimes be stranger than fiction.

STEDE BONNET: CHARLES TOWN'S GENTLEMAN PIRATE

O ver the years, nearly every major travel magazine in the United States and abroad has touted Charleston as the most gracious, polite city in America. Even one of its best-known pirates, Stede Bonnet, is widely remembered as a gentleman.

Few city tour guides fail to include at least a mention of Bonnet and his crew as they pass the memorial marker at the site where they are thought to have been executed at White Point Gardens. *(Oops, sorry, maybe that should have been prefaced with a spoiler alert!)* Okay, so now you know how the story ends. Still, some of its lesser-known details make the true story of Major Stede Bonnet, Charles Town's Gentleman Pirate, worth telling again in more depth.

Like many things relating to Charleston's history and culture, Stede Bonnet came to the Carolinas via Barbados, where he was born in 1688 to Edward and Sarah Bonnet, wealthy colonists who owned a sugar plantation of more than four hundred acres southeast of the island's capital, Bridge-town. Records from the island's Christ Church Parish confirm that the Bon-nets' first son, Stede, was christened there on July 29 of that year.

Little is known of Bonnet's youth, though he undoubtedly received a good education, as his contemporaries described him as "bookish," and at his sentencing, Judge Nicholas Trott referred to his liberal education.[1] Upon his father's death in 1694, Stede inherited the family's plantation while still a child, in accord with Barbadians' tradition of primogeniture, the system whereby the first son inherits virtually everything and subsequent sons usually go into the military or ministry or perhaps travel to England to read law. Once Stede came of age, he served honorably, if not distinguishably, in the Barbadian militia during Queen Anne's War, attaining the rank of major, an accomplishment perhaps owing as much to his status as a landowner as his skill as a soldier.

According to parish records in Bridgetown, Bonnet married Mary Allamby on November 21, 1709, and they had four children together: Allamby, Edward, Stede, and Mary. (Mary's daughter, Stede's granddaughter, would grow up to marry Gen. Robert Haynes, who served for thirty-six years as Speaker of the Barbadian Assembly.)

Yet by 1717, Bonnet had apparently hit what *Smithsonian* magazine has referred to as "the worst midlife crisis on record."[2] No one knows exactly why the wealthy, educated gentleman woke up one morning and decided to become a pirate, but most hypotheses revolve around the possibility that Mrs. Bonnet had turned out to be a bit of a shrew. According to Capt. Charles Johnson, author of *A General History of the Robberies and Murders of the most notorious Pyrates*, Mary's nagging and the "[d]iscomforts he found in a married State" drove Bonnet to abandon his family and turn to a life of piracy.[3] Others have suggested financial problems or the death of one of his children may have played a part in his decision. One North Carolina researcher postulates that Bonnet was probably a Jacobite, supporting James Stuart as the true King of Britain rather than the German-born George I, and so he made his decision either out of loyalty to James or merely in opposition to authority in general.[4]

Whether it was some combination of these factors or others, we'll never know. But whatever the reason, and despite the fact that he had no sailing experience whatsoever, Bonnet had his attorneys draw up the necessary legal papers turning management of his plantation over to his wife and two trusted friends.[5]

Not only was Bonnet not a sailor, he didn't seem to know much about the pirate business at all. As anyone worth his salt knows, pirates begin their criminal careers by first commandeering a ship through force of arms and pressing its crew into service under their command. Bonnet's approach to his new career employed a simpler approach: He bought a sloop at a reasonably fair price; outfitted it with ten fine guns, which he paid for out of his own savings; and posted advertisement circulars in the local pubs that he was hiring a crew of seventy men, promising them a decent day's wage for a decent day's work. Again, not really the way of most pirates, who earned their living by sacking, stealing, kidnapping, and murder.

Nevertheless, naming his new sloop the *Revenge* (perhaps an homage to Mrs. Bonnet, though also not an uncommon name among pirate ships of the day), Bonnet and his crew quietly slipped out of Bridgetown harbor under cover of night and set off for a life of adventure.

Despite now being a pirate, Bonnet maintained his cultivated sense of good taste, fashion, and manners. He dressed in fine clothes, was well groomed, and usually wore a powdered periwig. Upon meeting Bonnet for the first time, his contemporaries said they could tell immediately by his bearing and speech that he was well educated, witty, and refined—qualities that earned him the nickname "The Gentleman Pirate." Yet, lest anyone write Bonnet off completely as a dandy, it is worth noting that he was one of the very few captains who ever actually required prisoners to walk the proverbial plank,[6] a mostly mythical practice again promulgated by Captain Johnson's dramatized *History of the Pyrates*.

Despite Bonnet's eccentricities and inexperience, by late summer of 1717, he and his crew had begun to develop a reputation as a threatening presence along America's mid-Atlantic coast. Though not hugely successful compared to other legendary pirates, they did seize a respectable number of ships and plunder, including the *Anne* of Glasgow, the *Endeavor* of Bristol, the *Young* of Leeds, and the *Turbes* from Barbados. While the crews of the first three boats were mercifully set ashore on small islands to fend for their survival, the *Turbes* was burned at sea, establishing Bonnet's propensity to burn most of the ships he captured sailing under a Barbadian flag. No reliable sources establish his reasons for doing that, but some suggest it was because he didn't want word of his marauding deeds to get back to his family and friends in Barbados.[7]

Bonnet soon turned toward Charles Town's harbor, where he commandeered two more ships coming to trade with the port colony, after which

Though no authenticated images of the dapper Stede Bonnet exist, this engraving of him and his Jolly Roger flag first appeared in *A General History of the Robberies and Murders of the Most Notorious Pyrates*, written by Capt. Charles Johnson in 1724. *WikiMedia Commons*

he put into a North Carolina cove to make repairs to the *Revenge*. Around this time, Bonnet was wounded in an encounter with a Spanish ship, and his crew began to express concerns about their captain's leadership qualities. Nevertheless, once its repairs were completed, the *Revenge* headed south to a popular pirate hangout in Honduras for a little R & R, where their future would take a new turn.

While anchored in Honduras, the dissatisfied grumblings of Bonnet's crew came to the attention of another sea captain vacationing in that port, one Edward Teach, aka Blackbeard, one of the fiercest pirates in history. Though the two men were clearly cut from different cloth, Teach found his rather bonny comrade captain to be a man of charm and interest. Rather than seize the *Revenge* outright for himself, Blackbeard suggested that one of his most trusted crewmen should take command of Bonnet's ship, while Bonnet joined him as a guest aboard his own ship and focused on recuperating from the wound he had received in his confrontation with the Spanish galleon. Some accounts of their early days together note that Bonnet was happy to have a respite from his captain's duty, often sleeping late before appearing on deck still dressed in his nightgown and reading one of the books from the personal library he carried with him on his travels.[8] Other accounts claim Bonnet was virtually a prisoner aboard Blackbeard's ship, though treated with collegial respect. The truth probably lies somewhere between the two stories.

Either way, during their travels together over the next few months, they captured another dozen or so ships, bringing in a generous haul of booty even by pirate standards of the day. One of their notable capers together was a blockade of Charles Town Harbor in late May or early June of 1718, during which they seized eight or nine local ships along with a number of prominent Charlestonians who were onboard them, including Samuel Wragg, a member of the South Carolina Commons House of Assembly, and his young son, William.

Rather than demanding a monetary ransom as was customary, however, Blackbeard demanded a chest of various medicines, as he had a number of sick and injured crew members.[9] If the medicines weren't delivered within two days, the pirates threatened, they would begin sending the heads of the captives back to shore, starting with the Wraggs. Charles Town's proprietary governor, Robert Johnson, met their demands, and the captives were released unharmed. Still, it was a victory that did not sit well with Governor Johnson.

Bonnet and Blackbeard's partnership, however, was short-lived, though reasons for their split vary according to one's source. Some say that upon a return trip to North Carolina, as Bonnet went ashore, Blackbeard stripped the *Revenge,* stole all of its booty for himself, and stranded many of Bonnet's crew on a nearby island without food or supplies. Understandably angry, Bonnet resumed command of his ship, rescued his crew, and, according to this version of the tale, struck out for the high seas seeking revenge against Blackbeard. If indeed that was the case, it's probably fortunate for Bonnet that he never caught up with his former partner.

Other sources say dissension among their respective crews simply led the two captains to agree that parting would be best. Either way, it seems clear that the reputedly vicious Blackbeard had an unusual soft spot for his cultured gentleman colleague.

Upon his parting with Blackbeard, Bonnet began thinking about an early retirement. The thought became even more attractive when he heard that Proprietary Governor Charles Eden of the northern Carolina colony (the colony began to identify as North and South Carolina around 1712, though the division was not recognized as official until 1729) was granting the King's Pardon to pirates who voluntarily agreed to lay down their arms, surrender their ships, and settle down to a more traditional mercantile or agrarian lifestyle.

But then another, even better, option presented itself. A new war, the War of the Quadruple Alliance, had broken out in Europe, this time pitting the British and French against the Spanish and Jacobites, which meant that Britain, France, and Spain were again awarding governmentally sanctioned licenses for the legal privateering of foreign ships. That was just too good a deal to pass up. Bonnet refitted the *Revenge,* applied for his British license, and set out again for adventure on the high seas.

Meanwhile, back in Charles Town, Proprietary Governor Robert Johnson, still sensitive to the humiliation he had suffered at the hands of Blackbeard and Bonnet earlier that year regarding the medical supplies, called for an end to piracy and commissioned Col. William Rhett to track down and arrest any pirates, even those alleging to be legally sanctioned privateers, that he could find. Rhett quickly refitted two of his merchant ships, the *Henry* and the *Sea Nymph*, with eight powerful guns each and a crew of about 125 men between them. The ships passed out of Charles Town Harbor in August 1718, not seeking Bonnet per se, but hoping to capture another of Charles Town's notorious pirates, Charles Vane. Vane successfully escaped Rhett

Col. William Rhett built his double tenement residence in 1712, about six years before he set out to capture Stede Bonnet. The house on Hasell Street remains a private residence today. *Library of Congress*

(this time), but the voyage nevertheless promised to yield the desired results when Rhett learned that a pirate ship, along with two "prizes" (smaller captured sloops), had put into the Cape Fear River to make repairs. Initially, Rhett did not know that ship was Bonnet's *Revenge*, which by this time he had rechristened the *Royal James*. (Some pirate authorities have noted that it is considered bad luck to rename a ship, perhaps another amateur error on Bonnet's part.)

On September 26, 1718, Rhett entered the mouth of the Cape Fear River, and it didn't take long before things took an unfortunate turn for the Carolinians. Neither Rhett nor his pilots were familiar with the inlet's shallow waters, which were dotted with sandbars left and right. Soon both his ships ran aground, just as they could just see the mast tips of Bonnet's *Royal James* peeking above the treetops around a bend farther upriver. Nevertheless, they were stuck.

It would be at least six hours, nearly midnight, before the rising tide would begin bringing the Carolinians' ships afloat again, though even then, continuing forward in the unknown darkness would pose a ridiculous risk. But one thing they knew regardless of what happened with the timing and the tides, Bonnet and the *Royal James* were not getting out of that inlet

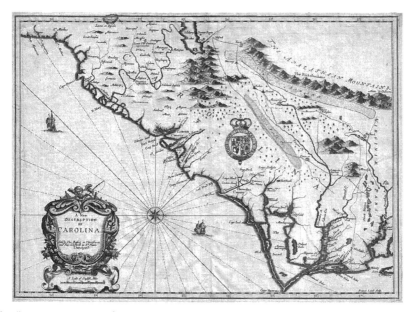

This "New Description of Carolina" shows both the Charles Town colony and the Cape Fear River before Carolina was divided into two colonies. *WikiMedia Commons*

without having to go around them. As midnight's tide began to refloat the two Carolina ships, Rhett's crew prepared for battle.

Though Rhett had hoped to surprise Bonnet, that hope was dashed. Long before dark, Bonnet's scouts had identified Rhett's well-armed ships as pirate hunters. And so, like those on Rhett's boats, Bonnet's men also began preparing for the inevitable conflict. As the sun rose the next morning, Rhett could see Bonnet's sails being raised for what was going to be a very close encounter at the river's mouth.

Bonnet's strategy was to hit Rhett hard enough, fast enough, to drive him backward into the open water of the Atlantic, where there was a chance for escape.[10] Anticipating the move, Rhett repositioned his ships and dropped anchor, hoping that between his two ships, they could forcefully maneuver Bonnet's *Royal James* closer to the river's shore and its shallow waters.

Coming together, the three ships began blasting one another broadside as fast as they could reload the cannons. Rhett's strategy worked: The *Royal*

James bottomed out as it passed too near the shoreline in its effort to escape the river's mouth.

But the real battle was just beginning. In the process of maneuvering the *Royal James*, Rhett's ships also grounded again. The *Sea Nymph*, which had been moving into position to block the *Royal James*'s escape into open waters, came to rest upon a sandbar downriver, effectively out of cannon range. On the other extreme, Rhett's *Henry* grounded nearly against the *Royal James,* so close that the two crews were within pistol range. Both ships careened inland, an angle that provided shelter for Bonnet's crew, as its deck was tilted toward the land, exposing its hull to the enemy. Just downriver of the *Royal James*, the same position exposed the *Henry*'s men on the inclined deck, directly in the pirates' line of small arms fire. So assured of their victory given this advantage, the pirates began chanting derisions at the Carolinians, just a stone's throw away. As the pirates rained bullets around them, the *Henry*'s crew took shelter as best they could before gallantly dodging the pistol shots well enough to reload their cannon and fire several large, heavy balls into Bonnet's exposed hull.

Hours passed this way. Somewhere between five and six of them actually, as the tide again shifted its flow. At some point the sailors on all three ships must have anticipated what would happen next, thanks to nature's every-day, relentless routine. As the tide began flowing back into the river, first the *Sea Nymph* and then the *Henry* righted and began to float, shortly before the *Royal James*'s hull, now riddled with cannon ball holes, struggled without hope to rise above the river's bed. Bonnet's well-recognized Jolly Roger came down as his crew raised their white flag, surrendered unconditionally, and begged for mercy. It was one of the bloodiest and most definitive battles in pirate history.

Colonel Rhett sailed back into Charles Town Harbor with his prisoners amid cheers on October 3, 1718. After two days at anchor, he presented about three dozen captive pirates (reports vary) to Marshal Nathaniel Partridge of Charles Town's City Guard. The colony had not yet built a prison, so prisoners were often held at Marshal Partridge's house at the corner of Tradd and Church Streets, though Dr. Nicholas Butler, historian at the Charleston County Public Library, notes that old maps show Partridge owned several properties in and around the city, any of which could have served as their holding site.[11] Still, around three dozen prisoners were more than his residence(s) could accommodate, so the prisoners were crowded into a civic building known as the Watch House.

More hospitable accommodations, however, were made for Stede Bonnet himself. As a former officer of the Barbadian militia and scion of the landed gentry, he was afforded private accommodations in the marshal's home, giving his word as a gentleman that he would not try to escape. Generally speaking, he received the normal courtesies of any other house guest.

Two of Bonnet's crew, David Herriot, his navigator, and Ignatius Pell, his boatswain, agreed to testify against their comrades, and so were reassigned from the Watch House to await trial with Bonnet at the marshal's residence. Though courtesy was the order of the day, two guards were nevertheless posted outside the residence to ensure that Bonnet's word as a gentleman would indeed be reliable. As Bonnet and his men awaited trial, many of the marshal's neighbors and associates would stop by the house to meet the infamous pirate. Local lore holds that Bonnet even attended balls and other social events, charming everyone in Charles Town, especially the ladies, with his suave and debonair demeanor. He became quite popular and, like some hardened criminals today, garnered quite a fan base among the colony's citizens.

Meanwhile, the rest of the crew stood trial before the presiding judge of the South Carolina Court of Vice-Admiralty, Nicholas Trott. Fortunately, a nearly complete transcript of Charles Town's pirate trials of 1718 was kept and even published in London in 1719 as *The Tryals of Major Stede Bonnet, and Other Pirates.* In his podcasts, Dr. Butler quotes extensively from these records, which became accessible to the public when they were transcribed and published digitally by the Library of Congress.[12]

Contrary to one's assumption, there was not a single, large trial for Bonnet and his crew but eleven smaller trials held in rapid succession. Dr. Butler attributes one reason for this to be that the trials were held in the residence of a Mr. Vanvelsen, who lived next door to Marshal Partridge's Tradd Street residence, in a space that would not accommodate all of the accused pirates at once.

THE

TRYALS

O F

Major *STEDE BONNET*,

AND OTHER

PIRATES,

VIZ.

Robert Tucker,	*Samuel Booth,*	*Henry Virgin,*
Edward Robinson,	*William Hewet,*	*James Robbins,*
Neal Paterson,	*John Levit,*	*James Mullet* alias *Millet,*
William Scot,	*William Eddy* alias *Nedy,*	*Thomas Price,*
Job Bayley,	*Alexander Annand,*	*John Lopez,*
John-William Smith,	*George Ross,*	*Zachariah Long,*
Thomas Carman,	*George Dunkin,*	*James Wilson,*
John Thomas,	*John Ridge,*	*John Brierly,* and
William Morrison,	*Matthew King,*	*Robert Boyd.*
William Livers alias *Evis,*	*Daniel Perry,*	

Who were all condemn'd for PIRACY.

AS ALSO

The TRYALS of *Thomas Nichols, Rowland Sharp, Jonathan Clarke,* and *Thomas Gerrat,* for PIRACY, who were Acquitted.

AT THE

Admiralty Sessions held at *Charles-Town,* in the Province of *South Carolina,* on Tuesday the 28th of *October,* 1718. and by several Adjournments continued to Wednesday the 12th of *November,* following.

To which is Prefix'd,

An ACCOUNT of the Taking of the said Major *BONNET,* and the rest of the PIRATES.

LONDON:

Printed for BENJ. COWSE at the *Rose* and *Crown* in *St. Paul's Church-Yard.* M. DCC. XIX.

Transcripts from *The Tryals of Major Stede Bonnet, and Other Pirates* are available for public viewing through the Library of Congress Digital Collections. *Library of Congress*

In this era of colonial jurisprudence, there were no lawyers to advise the accused. Each crewman spoke on his own behalf, with about as much expertise in the legal system as Bonnet had in seafaring when he first became a pirate. All but three (James Wilson, Daniel Perry, and John Levit) pleaded innocent, claiming they had been forced into a life of crime by Bonnet, a rather dubious claim given how unconventionally he had hired his first crew with the promise of good wages.

That, along with the testimony of state's witness Ignatius Pell, Bonnet's boatswain, sealed their fate. All except Pell and four others, who offered sufficient evidence to support their claim of being forced into a life of piracy against their will, were found guilty and sentenced to be hanged.

As the condemned crew's trials began wrapping up next door, Bonnet and Herriot "read the room," as it were, and went back on their word as gentlemen and escaped. Bonnet would later claim that they had received help from some of the well-to-do colonists in the town who had befriended him during his confinement at the marshal's, though he did not name anyone specifically.[13] Local lore claims that the two escaped by raiding Mrs. Partridge's closet (perhaps even with her consent) and dressing as women to pass through the streets unnoticed, yet no documentation has ever given credence to the story. Pell, the boatswain, had stayed behind, wisely leaving his fate to the clemency of the colonial judicial system.

Upon hearing news of the escape, Governor Johnson was about as unhappy as governors get. He promised a generous reward, some sources say seven hundred pounds (nearly $184,000 in today's US dollars), to anyone who returned the escapees to custody. Mr. Partridge was promptly replaced as city marshal.

Bonnet had planned his escape well enough to have a boat waiting for them, but his general lack of seamanship was once again his downfall: He failed to have his accomplices supply the escape boat with food, water, or other necessary provisions. In addition, the two escapees immediately set sail for North Carolina with the wind in their face. Needless to say, it wasn't long before they were forced to return to Sullivan's Island for supplies and to plan a new getaway strategy, with consideration given to which way the wind was blowing.

Before they could finalize their new plans, however, they were spotted by someone who, though his or her name has been lost to history, informed Colonel Rhett that Bonnet and Herriot were hiding within Sullivan's Island's thick myrtle forest along the harbor's northern shore. Following a diligent search, Rhett's men found them on November 5, about two weeks after their escape. In the confrontation that followed their discovery, Herriot was mortally wounded. Bonnet, true to style, called upon his charm and charisma to again divert further fire or violence upon his person, and Rhett safely returned him to the new marshal's custody the next morning.

Two days later, on November 8, twenty-nine of Bonnet's crew were hanged at White Point Garden. Some sources, though none substantial enough to be considered definitive, say they were left dangling from the trees for several days before being cut down and buried below the high-water mark, where, of course, their bodies would be uncovered by the tides and wash around the city's perimeter for a while longer. Governor Johnson wanted to make clear that pirates would no longer be tolerated in Charles Town, and that anyone considering the trade should think again.

Two days later, after the mass execution of his crew, Bonnet himself was brought to trial. Pleading not guilty to the first charge, he called upon all of his gentlemanly manners to appeal to the judge's mercy and blamed all of his misdeeds on Blackbeard. Having failed to achieve an innocent verdict with that strategy, he switched tactics during his second trial and pleaded guilty, hoping his repentance and a remorseful display would find favor in the judge's eyes. That effort also failed, and Judge Trott pronounced his sentence of death by hanging. Governor Johnson set the date of his execution for December 10.

Bonnet spent the twenty-eight days between his sentencing and execution in "abject terror and agony,"[14] leaving no stone unturned in seeking a reprieve. He wrote to Governor Johnson, saying, "I once more beg for the Lord's Sake, dear Sir, that as you are a Christian, you will be as charitable as to have Mercy and Compassion on my miserable Soul, but too newly awakened from a Habit of Sin to entertain so confident Hopes and Assurances of my blessed Jesus, as is necessary to reconcile me to so speedy a Death; wherefore as my Life, Blood, Reputation of my Family, and future happy State lies entirely at your Disposal, I implore you to consider me with a Christian and charitable Heart, and determine mercifully of me that I may ever acknowledge and esteem you next to God, my Saviour; and oblige me ever to pray that our heavenly Father will also forgive your Trespasses."[15]

Bonnet begged and appealed to anyone who would listen, promising to lead a reformed life. Many Charlestonians who formerly feared him began to warm to his charm and gentlemanly persona. Some sent letters of support to Governor Johnson on his behalf, asking if not for a pardon, at least for a commutation of the death penalty. Even Colonel Rhett, of all people, was moved by Bonnet's pleas and asked Governor Johnson if he could take Bonnet to England for his case to be reviewed there. But Johnson was resolute in his decision. No mercy was shown.

On December 10, Stede Bonnet, near fainting according to news reports, had to be assisted on his walk to the gallows. One observer was quoted as saying, "he was scarce sensible when he came to the place of execution."[16] A news report noted that "[s]ome in the crowd reportedly felt pity as the once proud man, with dropping head, walked up to the gallows, with shackled hands holding a bouquet" of flowers.[17] The noose was placed and the floor of the gallows dropped. It had been less than two years since Bonnet had left Barbados on his newly purchased *Revenge*.

Like his fellows, Bonnet may well have been buried in the pluff mud below the high-tide mark, which would soon wash away all traces of the gentleman whose name only lives on today because of his dream to be a pirate. With Bonnet's death, the golden age of piracy was over in Charles Town.

ANNE BONNY: THE REMARKABLE ADVENTURES OF A FEMALE PYRATE

Determining factual details about the life and death of Anne Bonny is about as elusive as finding a chest of buried treasure could ever be. Dr. Nicholas Butler, historian at the Charleston County Public Library, notes that only two reliable historic records about her life exist today. One is a proclamation by Bahamian Governor Woodes Rogers made September 5, 1720, and published in the *Boston Gazette,* naming Bonny and Mary Read among his "Most Wanted Pirates" list and declaring them "Enemies to the Crown of Great Britain and to be so treated and deem'd by all His Majesty's subjects."[1] The second source is the record of her trial. Though scant, these two documents alone confirm that Anne Bonny's life was one of murder, greed, sex, and violence, and that she was among the more barbaric killers of her day.

Pretty much the rest of the story surrounding Bonny's life comes to us from *A General History of the Pyrates, with the remarkable Actions and Adventures of the Two Female Pyrates Mary Read and Anne Bonny,* written in 1724, four years after Bonny's mysterious disappearance, by Capt. Charles Johnson, believed by many to be a pen name for fiction writer Daniel Defoe, author of *Robinson Crusoe.*[2] Though few people have ever heard of Captain Johnson's book, it has essentially served as the foundation from which today's stereotypes and movie images of the swashbuckling pirate have evolved.

Copper engraving by Benjamin Cole (1695–1766). "Ann Bonny and Mary Read convicted of Piracy Novr. 28th. 1720 at a Court of Vice Admiralty held at St. Jago de la Vega in an Island of Jamaica." Found in Johnson, Charles (1724), *A General History of the Pyrates: From Their First Rise and Settlement in the Island of Providence, to the Present Time. With the Remarkable Actions and Adventures of the Two Female Pyrates Mary Read and Anne Bonny*, second edition. London: T. Warner, plate facing p. 157. *WikiMedia Commons*

Other details of Bonny's life have come to us through undocumented sources that have surely been embellished over three centuries of retelling. Yet even with an appreciation that most of the lurid details are the product of unreliable oral histories, the basic truth of Anne Bonny's life remains a story worth telling—for it captures the courage and bravado of a colonial-era woman who had the chutzpah to escape the narrow, deferential role defined for women of her day. She challenged the long-held superstition that allowing a woman onboard ship brought bad luck—at least as long as you didn't cross her. The veracity of the following details about Anne's life, outside of Governor Rogers's proclamation and her subsequent trial, is left to the reader's discretion.

Johnson's popular version of the story goes that even Anne's birth was scandalous. Born around 1700 near Cork, Ireland, she was said to be the illegitimate daughter of a married lawyer (usually named as William

McCormack) and his maid, Mary "Peg" Brennan. Though various stories of Peg's pregnancy and Anne's birth abound, suffice it to say the new baby caused problems (understandably) in the McCormacks' marriage, which resulted in his leaving Ireland with his mistress and their daughter to escape the scandal's fallout.

Colonial Charles Town was an ideal place for a man like McCormack (who at this point may have shortened his name to Cormac) to make a new start. He tried his hand at several careers, but in the end found his niche as a merchant. He was quite successful and soon accumulated enough wealth to buy a plantation and ensure that Anne would have the opportunity to count herself among the colony's social elite when the time came for her debut and marriage prospects.

But it was not to be. Oral histories claim that Peg died while Anne was still a child, most suggest around twelve years old, and Anne became a rebellious, unruly teenager. She had no interest in availing herself of the educational opportunities her father's wealth afforded her, and she was quick to pick a fight. Some accounts claim that at the young age of thirteen, Anne stabbed one of the family's enslaved women and seriously injured a young man who exercised the poor judgment of making advances her way.[3]

Anne also made it clear that she had no interest in caring for a husband and raising children, pretty much the only role open to a young woman of her station. She developed a taste for alcohol and began spending time in town near the docks, associating with men and women of dubious character. To her father's hurt and embarrassment, Anne seemed to relish the bad reputation she was developing. The more her father tried to set her life back on the right track, the more she rebelled, eventually eloping with a penniless young pirate named James Bonny, of whom her father vehemently disapproved. It was the last straw for Cormac. He disowned his daughter and declared that she was on her own.[4]

Sometime between 1714 and 1718, James and Anne Bonny sought refuge in Nassau, the capital of New Providence Island in the Bahamas and a thief's sanctuary often referred to as the Republic of Pirates. Anne flourished in this exciting and dangerous environment, spending much of her time befriending (and undoubtedly seducing) notorious characters in local taverns. Johnson records in his *General History* that Anne was "not altogether so reserved in point of Chastity," noting that James once found his wife "lying in a hammock with another man."[5]

Even as Anne flourished in Nassau, James did not. He took a few jobs as a privateer, working on ships authorized by the government to seize and rob ships of other nations. A pirate ship, by contrast, was not authorized by any nation and pilfered solely for its own profit. James's exploits as a privateer were unremarkable, and he was finding it hard to support his wife in the style she expected. To earn more money, James embarked on a second career: He became an informant for the Bahamas' first royal governor, Woodes Rogers (1679–1732), betraying his former colleagues and collecting the bounties on their heads.

Anne was disgusted by James's betrayals of their cronies. With the help of a popular gay reformed pirate-turned-bordello-owner named Pierre (a character perhaps more made-for-TV than historical), she left James and became involved with a number of other men. One, Capt. John "Calico Jack" Rackham, was perhaps the love of Anne's life, if you use the term loosely enough. Rackham was an Irish buccaneer who had come to Nassau seeking asylum under Governor Rogers's promise of amnesty for those who turned themselves in with a promise to give up piracy. He earned his fashionable nickname "Calico Jack" for his flamboyant, almost effeminate, clothing style.

James Bonny eventually caught up with his estranged wife and dragged her before Governor Rogers on charges of infidelity and marital desertion, both felonies. Rackham offered Rogers a monetary settlement (read "bribe") to release her, but the governor nevertheless sided with his old informant, ordering Anne to return home to James or be flogged. Again, details of the oral traditions vary, but one way or another, Anne and Calico Jack escaped from the island and the governor's sentence. At this point, she couldn't return to her father in Charles Town, nor could she continue living in Nassau, so she convinced Calico Jack to return to piracy with her as his partner.

Anne and Jack commandeered a sloop and, after recruiting a crew, began mercilessly raiding small vessels along the coast of Jamaica. In addition to themselves, their crew included eleven men and another woman,

Mary Read. Anne and Mary presumably became fast friends, sharing a love for brutality and adventure. More salacious undocumented accounts have the two bawdy, cross-dressing women also being involved in a bisexual relationship with Jack and others.[6] Another popular but undocumented story claims that when Anne became pregnant, Rackham dropped her off on the island of Cuba, where she gave birth, abandoned the baby (hopefully to some charitable soul), and headed back out to sea.

Leaving Captain Johnson's flair for storytelling aside now for a moment, what we can document from historical records is that Anne Bonny seemed born to be a pirate. Testimony at her trial shows that she fought, drank, and swore with the best of them. She knew how to handle herself with both a cutlass and pistol, was fierce in battle, and never showed mercy. When it came time to board a victimized vessel, she was among the first over the rail.[7] Though she sometimes disguised herself, dressing as a man when she was fighting, she also lived openly onboard ship as Rackham's sexually provocative lover.

Governor Rogers's proclamation in the *Boston Gazette* confirms that Anne and Rackham stole the *William*, a sloop with four cannons and two swivel guns, which allowed for a wider, more effective field of aim.

In his proclamation, Governor Rogers identified eight of the pirates by name, including Rackham, Bonny, and Read, avowing that the "Pirates Swear Destruction to all those who belong to this island."[8] His royal colleague, Governor Sir Nicholas Lawes of Jamaica, commissioned a bounty hunter named Jonathan Barnet to bring in Rackham's crew, which he did about a month later. According to Johnson's *General History*, Rackham's men were sleeping off the previous evening's drunken celebration of a raid when Barnet slipped up on them. Bonny and Read, Johnson said, were the only two of the crew who put up a fight. Soon Barnet had the entire crew in chains and on their way back to face the authorities. Bonny was so angry with Rackham, Johnson relates, that she chided him, saying, "if he had fought like a man, he need not have been hanged like a dog."[9]

Returning to the documentable elements of Bonny's story as established at her trial,[10] she and Mary Read were tried in Jamaica on November 28, 1720. The men in their crew had already been tried and found guilty twelve days earlier on two of the four counts against them. The first witness, Dorothy Thomas, testified that the pirates stole her canoe filled with provisions, and that the two women "were there on Board the said sloop and wore Men's Jackets, and long Trouzers, and Handkerchiefs tied about the Heads; and that each of them had a Machet [machete] and Pistol in their Hands, and cursed and swore at the Men." She then testified that Anne and Mary had encouraged their colleagues to murder her "to prevent her coming against them," adding, "the Reason of her knowing and believing them to be women was, by the largeness of their Breasts."

Next, witness Capt. Thomas Spenlow swore that the two women were among the crew who commandeered his ship, along with its cargo of fifty rolls of tobacco, nine bags of pimiento (spices), and ten slaves. The next two witnesses, both Frenchmen speaking through an interpreter, testified that Rackham's crew, including Bonny and Read, captured them as they were hunting boar on Hispaniola. The women "did not seem to be kept or detain'd by Force, but of their own Free-Will and Content," they said.

Next, Capt. Thomas Dillon testified that he and his men abandoned ship when a "strange Sloop" fired upon his vessel, the *Mary*. As they rowed to shore, someone on Rackham's ship shouted that they were English and therefore their countrymen had nothing to fear. Dillon joined them aboard their ship where, he testified, he saw Anne Bonny holding a gun in each hand. The two women, he told the court, "were both very profligate, cursing and swearing much, and very ready and willing to do any Thing on Board."

Governor Lawes, who himself presided over the court proceedings, pronounced the verdict and sentencing: "You Mary Read, and Ann Bonny, alias Bonn, are to go from hence to the Place from whence you came, and from thence to the Place of Execution; where you shall be severally hang'd by the Neck, till you are severally Dead."

But Anne Bonny and Mary Read had one more card up their sleeve, Johnson says: They both called for mercy because they were pregnant, and the law did not allow the execution of a pregnant woman. Both were granted stays of their sentencing until after their babies were born.

Reliable parish records verify that Mary Read died in prison, close to what would have been her baby's due date. Most historians suggest that she probably died either in childbirth or from complications shortly thereafter. Her grave in Jamaica is marked simply with her name, "Mary Read, pirate," and dated April 28, 1721.[11]

After her stay of execution was granted, however, Anne Bonny simply disappeared from the historical record. Johnson's *General History* correctly notes that, unlike her fellow pirates, Mary Read included, history records no further mention of her fate.

In lieu of reliable records, all kinds of stories have come down to us about the ending of Anne Bonny's tale, the most popular being that she appealed to her father, promising to turn over a new leaf, and that he bribed authorities to return her to Charles Town, where she quietly married a respectable older gentleman, moved out of town, had children, and lived without further fanfare into her eighties.

Yet as recently as November 2020, a researcher found a grave in Jamaica, not far from Mary Read's, with a headstone reading "Ann Bonny," though the burial date is given as December 29, 1733, at least twelve years after her death sentence should have been carried out.[12] The lack of the *e* on the end of her first name lends a sense of legitimacy to this claim, as that is how the *Boston Gazette* spelled it in 1720; the *e* was not generally added to Anne until it was published that way in Johnson's *General History*. Others have speculated that the Ann Bonny buried here could be the pirate's daughter, who was born in prison. Or anybody for that matter. Who knows?

PART III
THE CODE DUELLO

B y today's standards, it may be hard for us to understand the rationale behind dueling, yet it was a commonly accepted tradition in Charleston's colonial and antebellum periods. Although practiced throughout the American colonies, it was most common in the South, particularly in and around Charleston. Most prevalently practiced during the first half of the nineteenth century, the tradition continued here until 1880, years after it had been outlawed elsewhere.[1] Dr. David Ramsay (1714–1815), respected physician and historian of the American Revolution, attributed Charlestonians' propensity for dueling to the city's climate, claiming that "warm weather and its attendant increase of bile in the stomach" generated "an irritable temper which made men say and do things thoughtlessly."[2] Indeed, most duels in Charleston were fought between the months of June and September, so perhaps he was on to something.

The code duello, or "affair of honor," was the way by which Southern gentlemen settled personal disputes and avenged insults made to one's self, family, or friends.[3] The issuance or acceptance of an invitation to duel was considered proof that a man was certain of the rightness of his claim, to the extent that he was willing to risk his life to prove it. Generally practiced by Charleston's plantation elite, to refuse a challenge was to sully one's honor, give credence to the accusations levied against you, and bring one's manhood into question. Refusing a challenge marked one as a coward, liar, and cad.

The most important thing to understand about the code duello is that it was a formalized protocol that ensured a couple of things, most of which, surprisingly, were actually put in place to minimize harm and save lives— as long as everyone played by the rules. Charleston's code, with guidelines adapted from an old Irish tradition, was formalized and published in 1838 by John Lyde Wilson (1784–1849), who served as the state's governor from 1822 to 1824. Wilson's guidelines were so specific, they even outlined participants' proper posture. Wilson believed dueling to be an effective mediation "as long as a manly independence and lofty personal pride . . . shall continue to exist."[4] The code provided options whereby men could avoid killing someone without loss of face, "when and how to issue appropriate challenges, and how to judge and reply to a note as being honorable or otherwise."[5] In addition to reiterating the old Irish code for dueling in an appendix, Wilson even included the sarcastic comments of a Massachusetts writer who noted that South Carolina would be held up as a paragon of gentility if judged by Irish standards. Wilson responded by ridiculing "[t]he idea of New England becoming a school for manners."[6]

Wilson was a man who understood the essence of the duel based on personal experience, and he was an ardent supporter of the process as a way to manage conflict. Following his term as governor, Wilson, who had served in the state senate prior to his election as governor, was again elected to that office in 1826. Yet before he could be reseated, he was accused of financial

Former governor John Lyde Wilson argued for the right of individuals to self-preservation and said the rules he laid out in his "Code of Honor" would save lives by preventing indiscriminate shooting. *The Internet Archive*

THE CODE OF HONOR;

OR

RULES FOR THE GOVERNMENT

OF

PRINCIPALS AND SECONDS

IN

DUELLING.

BY JOHN LYDE WILSON.

CHARLESTON, S. C.
PRINTED BY JAMES PHINNEY,
In the rear of 40 Broad-st.
1858.

mismanagement during his gubernatorial term by social activist and Charlestonian Thomas S. Grimké, brother of renowned (and in Charleston, infamous) abolitionists and suffragists Sarah and Angelina Grimké. Feeling that his honor had been impugned, Wilson challenged Grimké to a duel. Both sides, however, agreed to "set aside their Differences" after the funds in question were duly accounted for.[7] And that was essentially the upside of the dueling process: It provided ample opportunity to resolve an issue before punishments were wrought.

To begin, the code's ritualized process ensured that, first, all avenues of compromise and agreement between the parties had been exhausted before any random or passionate violence erupted in the heat of the moment. Because virtually every white man in town always carried firearms, the code helped prevent scenes such as those romanticized in popular Western movie barroom brawls. Dueling was considered an honorable mitigation tactic, and no social stigma was attached to its practice until the latter half of the nineteenth century.

When confronted by the fact that someone had been offended by the words or actions of another, it was the responsibility of the person who caused the offense to be the first to offer an apology. If the offender did not, and attempts at reconciliation failed to reach a satisfactory conclusion, then the offended party would issue a challenge.[8] Next, friends or family members known as "seconds" were appointed on behalf of each party to meet and try to work out an understanding, compromise, or retraction of the offense. Indeed, this step for friends to dispassionately talk through an issue was often an effective way to settle the dispute once the principals' tempers had abated, and everyone had sobered up, had a night or two to sleep on the matter, and gained some perspective. Indeed, such had been the case with Governor Wilson and Mr. Grimké.

However, failing to come to a mutual understanding moved the protocol to the next level. The challenge was declared and a date and location for the duel set.

A number of places in Charleston have earned a historical reputation for dueling. Duels were said to take place near the old colonial-era army barracks, today the iconic Cistern Yard of the College of Charleston on George Street;

at the Washington Race Course, just outside of town;[9] or within the city's narrow alleys, such as the old cow path later known as Philadelphia Alley.

The appointed date and time of the duel was another important safety factor. As weapons of the eighteenth and early nineteenth centuries were generally less "effective" at decisively killing someone than they are today, the code duello ensured that doctors and medical supplies would be on-site to lend immediate medical attention if necessary. Having an arranged duel at a set time and place also ensured that numerous witnesses would be present on behalf of both parties, and that the facts of what ensued would not be left to uninformed gossip or exaggeration (at least too much). The attendance of women and other family members, other than seconds, at these events was discouraged.

But perhaps most important of all, the code duello ensured that the duel was fought fairly and that neither side had an advantage over the other, regardless of wealth, connections, or social standing. One party selected a pair of weapons for the duel, nearly always pistols in Charleston; the other party had first pick of which of the equally paired weapons he would use. During the colonial period, early firearms such as muskets or "fowling pieces," similar to today's rifles, tended to be cumbersome to load and fire, as well as inaccurate. By the early 1820s, however, the invention of the percussion pistol allowed for faster, more accurate shooting and was the weapon of choice for most Lowcountry duelers.[10] As Charlestonians are historically prone to dramatically conspicuous consumption, over time such ornamented matched sets of dueling pistols became virtual works of art.

Once the weapons had been selected, the seconds' job was to inspect the weapons on-site and ensure that they were "clean" and that no trickery or deceit was involved. To ensure fairness, one of the seconds would flip a coin to determine which of them would give the "Ready, Fire!" command, while the other second selected in which directions the duelists would be facing. Duels were often fought in the early-morning hours to minimize the chance of having the sun's glare in one of the duelists' eyes.

As the principals, standing face-to-face, looked each other in the eye one last time in a calmer, more formal and controlled atmosphere several days following the offense, the code duello allowed both parties to give one hard

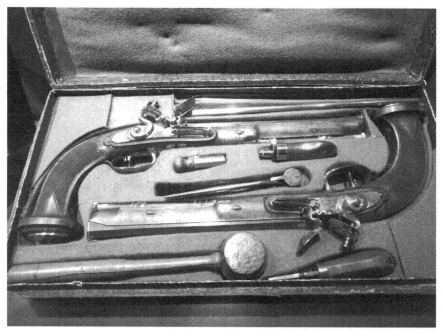

These single-shot flintlock dueling pistols, c. 1790s, were cumbersome to load and less accurate than nineteenth-century weaponry. *The Royal Ontario Museum, Toronto, Ontario, Canada*

last thought as to whether they were committed enough to their position to risk either causing or receiving serious injury or death. If so, then sometimes the parties would march off a set number of paces before turning to again face each other, but at other times they would simply take their positions at the spots upon which the seconds had already mutually agreed.

Finally, each party was allowed one shot, after which it was over, regardless of the outcome. According to Wilson's code, a wound received anywhere on the body of either principal would fulfill the requirements of the duel to restore each man's honor. If, however, one party was wounded, that party had the prerogative of calling for a second round of shots then and there. This, as one might guess, was a rare occurrence. In the worst of all cases, if one party failed to abide by the code's strict protocols or cheated in any way, the seconds had the right to shoot the offender themselves from the sidelines—and, in the very rarest of cases, each other.[11]

Here it is important to note that the code duello also provided a loophole that allowed both men to defend their honor to the point of risking their lives, but then to exercise the option of purposefully "missing" their one shot by shooting wide or into the ground, thus avoiding injury or death to either party. And so, given the safeguards ensured by the code duello, duels, while not uncommon, were rarely fought to the death. Such was the hope of Joseph Brown Ladd.

THE SAD DEMISE OF DR. JOSEPH BROWN LADD

William and Sarah Ladd's eldest son, Joseph, was born on a farm near Newport, Rhode Island, on July 7, 1764. Scant documentation of his early years survives other than the inscription on his mother's gravestone: *"Studious in infancy, he was a favourite of the muses, and highly promising in his profession of physick. . . . His writings . . . display genious [sic], which riper years might have led to eminence."[1]*

Joseph aspired to make his way in the world using his intellect rather than the toil of his hands, unlike his father, who was a farmer.[2] Realizing his son's potential, William Ladd allowed him time off from his chores to read and study at Redwood Library in Newport. That's probably where Joseph met and fell in love with Amanda, being "lovely to soul and to eye," an orphaned heiress "under the guardianship of mercenary relations, who finding the management of her estate a source of profit to themselves did not hesitate to sacrifice her happiness to their own interests."[3]

Joseph pursued Amanda passionately, writing copious love poems to her—though based on the woeful tones of his verse, perhaps she was less enthralled than he. Hoping to establish himself as a man of substance and thereby win Amanda's favor, Joseph began studying medicine at the age of fifteen with Dr. Isaac Senter.

Joseph soon proposed to Amanda, but her family disapproved—some suggest they did so because her marriage would mean they would lose control of Amanda's money. The family, who undoubtedly was well connected in Newport society, began spreading rumors besmirching Joseph's character and intentions, a plausible enough charge given the difference between their circumstances: "Not content with open opposition, they had recourse to calumnies, which, though groundless, were so ingeniously devised, and industriously bruited, as at one time to shake the confidence of some of his best friends."[4]

As the gossip spread, Dr. Senter suggested that it was time for Joseph to establish his own medical practice elsewhere, where he could get a fresh start. Senter asked his friend Gen. Nathanael Greene, a Revolutionary War hero who had campaigned in South Carolina, for advice. Thus, at Greene's suggestion, Joseph arrived in Charleston in 1783 to establish himself in hopes of convincing Amanda to join him here. He was just nineteen or twenty.[5]

Joseph soon found accommodations, renting a room from Fannie and Dellie Rose, spinster sisters who lived at 59 Church Street. Alas, it wasn't long before Joseph received news that Amanda had married another. Though heartbroken, his passion was unabated, and he continued to write poetry extolling his love for her.

The Thomas Rose House on Church Street, where Dr. Joseph Brown Ladd boarded with Fannie and Dellie Rose and reportedly died a week after suffering a gun wound received in a duel with Ralph Isaacs III. *Photo © Dr. Ken Dodds*

Otherwise, Ladd thrived in Charleston and was well liked, especially by his landladies, who were charmed by his habit of whistling as he went about his chores. The Rose sisters, well ensconced in Charleston society, introduced Ladd to their elite friends, many of whom became his clients. Governor William Moultrie even invited the doctor to address the Sons of Cincinnati at their 1785 Independence Day celebration.

Admired, esteemed, and beloved by a numerous circle in the highest ranks of society, and at the same time popular with the humbler class for his active benevolence; toiling incessantly at his profession, yet neglecting no opportunity to inform himself on subjects of interest to the scholar, philosopher, or politician; interesting himself in the important public questions of the day, particularly such as regarded the rising institutions of the commonwealth of which he had become a citizen; with a good constitution, temperate habits, and talents of the highest order, no young man perhaps ever had a fairer prospect of rising to eminence, usefulness, and high political distinction, than Dr. Ladd.[5]

Meanwhile, Ladd continued to write, publishing more than seventy poems.

According to undocumented oral history, Ladd, upon his arrival in Charles Town and undoubtedly looking a bit lost and naive, asked a stranger where he might find accommodations. A local attorney, Ralph Isaacs III, overheard their conversation and, recognizing the stranger as an unsavory character, intervened, perhaps saving Joseph from being robbed on his first day in town. The two became friends, though Isaacs began to feel a sense of jealousy and resentment toward his friend's quick rise within Charleston society. He accused Ladd of spending too much time with his new acquaintances at the expense of their friendship. Ladd sought to include Issacs in his activities, but Isaacs lacked the doctor's charm and failed to fit in with Charles Town's socially elite.

In the fall of 1786, as Dr. Ladd and Isaacs left a performance of Shakespeare's *Richard III* together, Isaacs complained about the shortcomings of an actress in the show. Ladd rose to her defense, and the evening ended on a sour note. Nursing a bruised ego, Isaacs published a letter in the October 12, 1786, *Charleston Morning News and Daily Advertiser*, declaring Ladd to be a scoundrel, social climber, and quack.[6] It was the opening salvo of a very public dispute.

To eighteenth-century Charlestonians, a man's honor was a matter of utmost concern—and in Charleston, these types of offenses were settled with pistols under the code duello. Ladd's friends insisted that this public offense must be answered, even though Joseph himself wished to just forget the matter.

Ladd responded to Isaacs's post by publishing one of his own, affirming his good character and noting that he was sorry they had ever been friends. To this, Isaacs threw down the gauntlet with a challenge to duel. Had Ladd not accepted, Isaacs's accusations would carry the weight of truth. Ladd had once before allowed unfounded accusations to run him out of town and away from his beloved, and he was unwilling to run a second time.

When the seconds were unable to reach an agreement, the duel was set for October 23. Ladd spent the preceding night writing to Amanda, noting that "friendly death may soon relieve my pain."[7] At dawn he and his witnesses arrived at Philadelphia Alley, a cow path connecting Cumberland and Queen Streets. The narrow alley, lined on both sides by the walls of residences and warehouses, ensured that no one could panic and run.

When a last effort at compromise failed, the opponents stood back-to-back and paced off before turning. As the challenged party, Ladd was allowed to take the first shot. He fired wide, trusting his former friend to do the same and they could call it a draw, according to the rules of the code duello.

Instead, Isaacs took aim and shot the doctor squarely in the kneecap. Ladd fell, screaming in agony, and was carried back to the Roses' house. There he suffered for ten days before succumbing to infection and blood loss on November 2. He was twenty-two years old.

Today some critics consider Ladd to be among the more accomplished poets of eighteenth-century America. One poem, "The Prospect of America," Ladd inscribed: "To the Second Fabius, His Excellency George Washington, Esq.," though the poem was never inventoried within Mount

Philadelphia Alley as seen today, where the duel between Dr. Joseph Brown Ladd and Ralph Isaacs III is believed to have taken place. Because the alley is bordered on both sides by buildings for nearly a block, its structure guaranteed that no one involved in the duel could panic and run. *Photo © Dr. Ken Dodds*

Vernon's library. In 1832, Ladd's sister, Elizabeth Ladd Haskins, published a collection of her brother's poems under the title *The literary remains of Joseph Brown Ladd, M.D.—A sketch of the Author's Life.*

And while the intent here is to share a historical account of the incident, suffice it to say that the historic marker erected by the Preservation Society of Charleston at 59 Church Street is the only one in this city—a city filled with ghost stories on nearly every street corner—to mention that the sound of whistling can still be heard on the dwelling's staircase.

PART IV
THE FAMOUS,
INFAMOUS, AND
MOSTLY FORGOTTEN

A s schoolchildren, most of us learned pretty much the same "officially sanctioned" version of American history: who won what battle; who our military and government leaders were; who discovered what; and, to some extent, who were the good guys and who were the bad guys that made stuff happen. Perhaps a better understanding and acceptance of the latter— that the good guys weren't always all good, nor were the bad guys always all bad—would go a long way toward healing the societal divisions we face in current times. Hopefully, that is one of the themes promulgated through the stories found herein.

Yet if history as an educational subject is worth its academic salt, as suggested by Peter N. Stearns, writing for the American Historical Association, it must accomplish two things. First, it must offer information that helps us understand how societies have functioned over time. Similarly, it must help us understand change and how we and the society in which we live today came to be what it is.[1] Only if we understand these two concepts can we hope to positively shape our futures.

Certainly there is an argument to be made for teaching children about the "big" names and events in history. Yet just as surely, there is also great value in understanding how the proletariat, the bourgeoisie, the unheralded minions, have likewise contributed to making us who we are today simply by surviving, evolving, and prospering (or not) while living ordinary lives during the historical times and challenges thrust upon them by the big names and events heralded in history textbooks.[2] This is especially true for women, the enslaved, the poor, and those who lost the battles in which they fought valiantly. After all that Eliza Lucas Pinckney accomplished in her lifetime as a businesswoman, inventor, and Patriot, today her headstone merely records her contributions to history as "the mother of Charles Cotesworth Pinckney and Thomas Pinckney, Patriots, Soldiers, Diplomats."[3]

Charleston, like any other American city or region, has its local heroes and villains with stories worth retelling. Some of them have had a national impact, such as Charles Pinckney (not to be confused with his cousin and Eliza's son Charles Cotesworth Pinckney), who penned the "Pinckney Draft" of the US Constitution, or Gen. William Moultrie, who handed the British their first major naval defeat of the American Revolution. Many scholars assert that had Moultrie not won the Battle of Sullivan's Island on June 28, 1776, no one would likely have been signing any documents proclaiming American freedom on July 4 (and yes, classroom history incorrectly teaches us that the Declaration of Independence was signed on July 4, a fait accompli).

Other stories primarily have only a local, but no less interesting and instructional, relevance. How did Sullivan's Island, today the wealthiest zip code in the state and one of the six wealthiest in the nation,[4] get its

William Moultrie (1730–1805) by artist Charles Willson Peale (1741–1827), c. 1782, oil on canvas. General Moultrie's successful rout of British Admiral Peter Parker's navy at the Battle of Sullivan's Island provided the impetus for delegates meeting in Philadelphia to adopt the Declaration of Independence. *WikiMedia Commons*

name? It was named for Francis O'Sullivan, who arrived in Charles Town aboard the first ship of permanent English setters in April 1670. (Somewhere along the way the O in O'Sullivan got dropped.) The boisterous Irishman was singled out as an outstanding individual among his contemporaries for a couple of reasons, and because of those reasons, he was assigned the vital task of manning the signal cannon at the mouth of Charles Town Harbor, alerting the new colonists to threats such as invading foreign ships or pirates. In fact, one might even credit O'Sullivan with saving the fledgling colony from an early extinction when he helped foil a Spanish attack in 1706. Yet his assignment to this then-remote island was not only a tribute to his bravery, military savvy, and keen survival skills; it also reflected the fact that O'Sullivan had developed a reputation as a "buggerer of small children," who parents wanted safely kept away from the colony's population center, as would we today.

How few people driving along Coming Street or Glebe Street, both bisecting the College of Charleston campus today, remember Affra Harleston Coming (c. 1640–1699), born into a moderately affluent family from Essex who fell on hard times after King Charles I's defeat? For reasons that will undoubtedly forever remain unknown, at about twenty-nine years old Affra indentured herself as a servant in order to book passage on the *Carolina*, leaving home, apparently alone, to seek a new beginning.[5] What could have driven her to be so courageous, risk so much, and go against so many norms of her time? Aboard ship she fell in love with and later married the captain's first mate, John Coming. Though John continued his career at sea for many years afterward, Affra swore she would never set foot on a ship again, nor did she. Instead, she literally carved out a home and developed a successful rice plantation from the wild wood thickets along the banks of the Cooper River, fighting the elements, snakes, alligators, epidemics, wild animals, and Native Americans—some friendly, others not—pretty much by herself along with a few enslaved workers.[6]

Now, more than three decades after its dedication, too few people today recall that downtown's Ralph H. Johnson Veterans Hospital was named for a marine reservist who was born in Charleston. Private First Class Johnson was serving in Vietnam when, in the early-morning hours of March 5, 1968, without hesitation or thought for self, he shouted a warning to his fellow soldiers before throwing himself on a grenade that had been lobbed into their foxhole. His body absorbed the entire impact of the blast. Johnson was killed instantly, even as he saved the lives of the others who shared his entrenchment.

And so it is perhaps not only the famous, but also the infamous and mostly forgotten, who have played critical roles in shaping our history. What follows are a few of those stories.[7]

Pfc. Ralph H. Johnson made the ultimate sacrifice for his country and his comrades by throwing himself on a live grenade in Vietnam.
US Department of Veterans Affairs

MARY FISHER BAYLEY CROSS: A WOMAN ON A MISSION

Born sometime around 1623, Mary Fisher began her life as a humble, illiterate housemaid working for Richard and Elizabeth Tomlinson in Selby, England, another seemingly anonymous soul among the millions history might easily have forgotten about long ago. Just goes to show the power of a good sermon.

Sometime around the end of 1651 or early 1652, George Fox, founder of the Religious Society of Friends, also known as Quakers, spent time as the Tomlinsons' houseguest, where he espoused his belief that God's divinity can be found within each of us and that Christians should experience a personal, one-on-one relationship with God rather than worship within the formal hierarchical structure of a state church system. Fox's personal charisma and evangelical message that all believers, regardless of gender or circumstances, are part of a universal priesthood resonated with Mary, who converted during his visit. Soon after, she joined Fox's Valiant Sixty, the first group of traveling missionaries whose mission was to spread the Quaker message throughout the world.

Within the first year of her conversion, it became clear that the humble housemaid had been transformed into the boldest of zealots when Mary publicly rebuked Selby's vicar after his Sunday sermon, saying, "Come downe, come downe, thou painted beast, come downe. Thou art but a hireling, and deluder of the people with thy lyes,"[1] a pronouncement that earned her about sixteen months' imprisonment in York Castle.

While there, she was in good company. Fellow Quaker inmates Elizabeth Wooten and Jane Holmes used their time in prison to teach Mary to read and write. Together they penned a pamphlet titled *False Prophets and False Teachers Described*, urging people to leave the established Anglican Church and embrace their Quaker tenets. This accomplishment earned them additional time as guests of York Castle.

Upon her release the following year, Mary and another Quaker, Elizabeth Williams, embarked on a journey to proselytize the southern regions of England. Together they traveled on foot to Cambridge, where they publicly challenged theology students at Sidney Sussex College, which they called "a cage of unclean birds, and the synagogue of Satan."[2] The young theologians responded to their denouncement by throwing stones at the women before the mayor had the two arrested, dragged to the local market, stripped to the waist, and "whipped at the market cross til the blood ran down their bodies"—the first documented beating of Quakers for their missionary efforts.[3]

Mary and Elizabeth spent the next two years, 1654 and 1655, traveling from village to village around the south of England, spreading the Quaker message and being imprisoned for it. If the punishments served no other purpose, they served to make Mary's convictions even stronger and her passionate desire to spread her message even further. Upon her release from prison in 1655, Mary and another friend, Ann Austin, decided it was time to take their message to the New World, and they boarded a boat to Barbados. Here, finally, their message was heard without remonstrations. Wealthy sugar planter Thomas Rous and his son John (who would later marry George Fox's daughter) were among the first to convert. Eventually the island would support five meetinghouses, making Barbados the hub of Quakerism in the New World.[4]

On July 11, 1656, Mary and Ann sailed into Boston Harbor, becoming the first Quakers in British North America. The Puritan deputy governor of the Massachusetts Bay Colony, Richard Bellingham, had already received word of their impending arrival and was prepared to silence their antichurch heresies. Before the women even left their ship, they were arrested and brusquely hauled ashore, where examiners stripped them naked in the public square and searched their bodies for any telltale signs of witchcraft. Ann Austin would later report that at least one of the supposedly female examiners was a man in disguise.[5] Their books and evangelical pamphlets were confiscated and burned and the women imprisoned.

To minimize the risk of their heresies reaching the ears of any curious local Puritans, Bellingham ordered that the doors and windows to the women's prison cell be securely boarded up. His intention for doing so, according to some historians, was to avoid a controversial execution by passively "allowing" them to starve, if God so deemed it.[6] Nevertheless, a local innkeeper, Nicholas Upsall, quietly bribed the guards five shillings a week to be allowed to smuggle food and water to the women and spend a short time speaking with them.

After about five weeks, with the women having "miraculously" survived without any known provisions, Deputy Governor Billingham determined it was best to put Mary and Ann back on the boat that had brought them over and send them back to Barbados. During their brief stay in New England, the only person they had seen or spoken to, secretly of course, was Nicholas Upsall, whom they successfully persuaded to become the first Quaker convert in the New World.

Mary continued her ministry in Barbados before returning to England in 1657, but her travels were far from over. Believing that God was calling her to minister to Turkish Sultan Mehmed IV, ruler of the Ottoman Empire and a dreaded figure in the imagination of Western European culture, Mary set out sometime around 1659, along with several companions, to find the sultan in the eastern Mediterranean. Tracking him down in Smyrna, the group's first attempt to arrange a meeting was obstructed by English diplomats. Discouraged after such a long, arduous trip, the rest of the group turned back, but not Mary. After covering six hundred miles, mostly on foot, she finally succeeded in gaining access to Mehmed IV's influential grand vizier Köprülü Mehmed Pasha, who was impressed by this passionate Englishwoman who proclaimed that she was an ambassador from the Most High God, come with a divine message for the sultan. The vizier arranged for a meeting with the sultan at his military camp near Adrianople.

Sultan Mehmed IV, oil on canvas, c. 1662, artist unknown. Mary Bayley Fisher Cross felt she had received a more Christian welcome from the Muslim Turks than she had from her Anglican countrymen or the New England Puritans. *WikiMedia Commons*

Mehmed IV listened attentively as Mary gave her witness through an interpreter, though no record of the conversation has been found. When she was done, he sat for a while, considering her words, and acknowledged that there was truth in what she said. Though he did not convert from Islam to Quakerism, Mehmed thanked Mary for traveling so far under such dangerous circumstances to bring him the message, and he offered a military escort to see her safely back to England on a royal barge. She declined, wished him well, and returned to England, satisfied that she had executed the task God had given her.

Mary later wrote of her experience with the Turks, comparing the treatment she received from these "barbarians" as much more compassionate than that she experienced with either her Anglican countrymen or the Boston Puritans, saying: "Now returned into England . . . have I borne my testimony for the Lord before the king unto whom I was sent, and he was very noble unto me and so were all that were about him . . . they do dread the name of God, many of them. . . .They are more near Truth than many nations; there is a love begot in me towards them which is endless, but this is my hope concerning them, that he who hath raised me to love them more than many others will also raise his seed in them unto which my love is. Nevertheless, though they be called Turks, the seed of them is near unto God, and their kindness hath in some measure been shown towards his servants."[7]

Not long after her return to England, Mary felt a new calling, this time to the more traditional role of wife and mother. While continuing her ministry in the area around Dorsetshire, she married William Bayley (sometimes spelled Baley or Baily), a Quaker sailor, minister, and author of religious pamphlets. Also converted to the faith by George Fox not long after Mary's conversion, Bayley had likewise suffered and spent time in prison for his efforts to promulgate the Quaker faith both at home and abroad. One account notes that when Bayley was arrested in London in 1662, an alderman began to beat him. Mary came to his rescue and was also knocked down twice, though she was obviously pregnant at the time.[8]

The Bayleys had three children: William Jr., Mary, and Susannah. William Bayley Sr. drowned at sea in 1675 on a voyage back to England from Barbados, leaving Mary a widow and single mother.

About three years later, Mary remarried, this time to John Cross (also Crosse), a Quaker shoemaker. The couple, along with her three children, moved in 1678 to Charles Town, known as a haven for those seeking freedom of worship. Mary seemed to have finally found a permanent home, and once she arrived in Charles Town, she ceased her missionary travels. No records indicate that she was ever again arrested or imprisoned.

Mary and John were active in the new colony's Quaker community, as borne out by a letter written in 1696 by Quaker missionary Richard Barrow to his wife back in England. In it he shares his experience of having been shipwrecked in Charles Town, where he received medical assistance and support from a kind woman "whose name you have heard of, a Yorkshire woman, born within two miles of York; her maiden name was Mary Fisher, she that spake to the great Turk, afterwards William Bayley's wife . . . she is a widow of a second husband, her name is now Mary Crosse."[9]

John Cross died in Charles Town in 1687, as did Mary in 1698. Mary began her will, written on August 8 and executed November 10, noting that she was "very sick and weak." Yet her will, as well as John's earlier one, show that the Cross family had fared well and prospered during their time in Charles Town. A map of the colony, perhaps made as early as 1680, shows the name of "Mrs. Crosse" on several town lots.

In her will, Mary left her son, William, a lot in town "whereon ye Great house stands," as well as fifty acres of land.[10] Though the house is long gone, one would find this lot today at the southeast corner of Meeting and Chalmers Streets, where the city's Fireproof Building, c. 1822, stands—today home of the South Carolina Historical Society Museum and Washington Park. In 1698 this would have been located just a block or two from Charles Town's Quaker meetinghouse, today occupied by the rear portion of the Mills House Hotel, fronting Meeting Street.

To her daughters, Mary and Susannah, both of whom had married well and had children of their own, Mary bequeathed several lots she noted were "situated near the Market Place," which at that time would have been in the area where Tradd, Elliott, and East Bay Streets exist today—a waterfront location overlooking the colony's Cooper River wharves. At least one of these lots included a house, which is where Mary probably was living at the time of her death.

In the latter part of the eighteenth century and into the nineteenth, Quakers were known for their abolitionist ideals and eventually became an unwelcome presence in Charles Town. Still, the issue of slavery had not galvanized the country this early in its history. Mary left to her daughter Mary a Native American slave girl named Rayner. Mary closed her will saying, "I recommend my soul to ye mercy of God my Creator hoping through the merrits of Jesus Christ to obtain forgiveness from all my sins and everlasting life."[11]

John and Mary Cross were buried in the Quaker graveyard surrounding the meetinghouse that stood on the south side of Queen Street between Meeting and King Streets. In 1967, just a year shy of the three-hundredth anniversary of Mary's death, Charleston County began construction of a new parking garage at the corner of King and Queen Streets. Many, though undoubtedly not all, of the Quaker graves there were dug up and the remains reinterred near the County Courthouse on Broad and Meeting Streets. Thus the final resting place of Mary Fisher Bayley Cross is uncertain today. All that remains of the Quaker churchyard is a mid-nineteenth-century iron fence that once surrounded it, and which now somewhat incongruently adorns a five-story parking garage.

AMERICA'S
FIRST CREMATION

When asked to name America's founding fathers, not nearly as many people remember the name Henry Laurens as they might George Washington, Thomas Jefferson, or Patrick Henry. But they should. A Charleston merchant and rice planter, Henry Laurens distinguished himself as a delegate to the Second Continental Congress, succeeding his much-better-remembered predecessor, John Hancock, as its president. It was during Laurens's tenure in that role, on November 15, 1777, that the Congress passed the Articles of Confederation, the agreement drawn up among the thirteen original states that served as America's first constitution.

Though he was a bit too old to actively serve on the front lines militarily by the time the Revolution got under way, Laurens nevertheless played a number of important roles as a statesman and ambassador. In the fall of 1779, the Congress sent Laurens as its minister to the Netherlands to seek that country's support in the colonies' fight against British rule. Though he was successful, during his voyage home his ship was unfortunately intercepted by the British. Laurens was captured and soon earned the distinction of being the only American ever held prisoner in the Tower of London. Fortunately he was released at the end of the war and went on to participate in drawing up the Treaty of Paris, the peace agreement with King George III that officially ended the American Revolution.

Visitors to Charleston who are looking for a deeper historical experience than just walking pleasantly along the Battery may visit the Laurens family's cemetery located on their beautiful former plantation, Mepkin, which

Portrait of Henry Laurens by Lemuel Francis Abbott (1760–
1802), oil on canvas, c. 1781. *WikiMedia Commons*

today serves as a tranquil abbey for a small group of Trappist monks along
the banks of the Cooper River. These days, however, following the wildly
successful Broadway production *Hamilton*, a lot of visitors are now more
interested in seeing the grave of Henry's son, John, a character who figures
prominently in the musical, than they are of seeing Henry's.

There's yet another, lesser-known way in which Henry Laurens made
American history. Though no reliable documentation exists, it is said that
when Henry was a child, his younger sister was pronounced dead from one
of the many fevers that plagued Charles Town's early years. As the family
made preparations for her funeral, her body lay in repose in the upstairs ball-
room of their house on East Bay Street, which faced the harbor. As the little

girl lay with her face turned toward the garden and the breezes from Charles Town Harbor, a storm blew up and rain from the open window splashed on her face. A servant saw her eyelids flutter and ran for help. The little girl recovered and lived to old age.

Whether or not the story is true, for the rest of his life, Laurens had an obsessive fear of being buried alive. In his will he directed his son: "as an indispensable duty that as soon as he conveniently can, after my decease, he cause my body to be wrapped in 12 yards of Tow Cloth and burnt until it be entirely and totally consumed and then collect my bones, deposit them wherever he shall think proper."[1]

When the time came, Laurens's family was hesitant to comply with this unorthodox, perhaps even "un-Christian," request. Thus, when he died, it was Laurens's slaves who gathered around his coffin on Mepkin's Bluff overlooking the Cooper River and complied with his request, the earliest documented cremation in America. His ashes are interred there in the family cemetery.

CARADEUX THE CRUEL

In a place and time defined by inhumanity and violence, Jean-Baptiste Caradeux stood out as a uniquely reprehensible individual. Though many of his Charleston descendants would recall him as a gallant defender of French values, the few others who remember him today most often do so for the brutality with which he treated his slaves.

Born February 24, 1742, at La Croix-des-Bouquets on the island colony of Saint-Domingue (what today we know as Haiti), Caradeux (also spelled Caradeuc) came from an ancient, noble French family. Few remaining records provide any account of his early years, except that he attended the finest schools in France, and on January 25, 1785, married Agathe Jeanne Louise de la Toison de Rocheblanche.[1]

Upon his return to Saint-Domingue, Caradeux established himself as a wealthy planter, owner of a large sugar refinery, and member of the Colonial Assembly. He was appointed Commander in Chief of the Royal Forces and rose to become Governor General of Saint-Domingue. He held the title Comte, similar in rank to the English title Count.

In contrast to the extreme poverty that defines Haiti today, in the late 1700s no other colony in the world turned as large a profit for its ruling class as did Saint-Domingue which produced a third of the world's sugar crop, half of its coffee demand, and numerous other sustaining crops as well.[2] Nearly fifteen hundred ships annually passed through the island's thirteen international ports. By the 1780s, Saint-Domingue's foreign trade equaled that of all the United States' ports added together. The profits Caradeux and his fellow elite planters made from the island's booming economy allowed them to live in luxury, riding in their splendid carriages to local orchestral productions, theaters, parks, military parades, and even a fashionable wax museum on the tropical island. British Prime Minister William Pitt (1759–1806), one of colonial Charles Town's favorite English politicians, called it "the Eden of the Western world."[3]

Like the great rice plantations of eighteenth- and nineteenth-century Charleston, Saint-Domingue's vast wealth was dependent on a half million enslaved Africans and their descendants whose lives were defined by toiling from sunup to sundown in the island nation's intense heat and humidity; digging and planting sugar cane in swamps infested with biting, disease-carrying insects; hauling eighty-pound baskets of manure to fertilize fields; and the backbreaking pain of bending over all day to slash the cane at its base during harvest time.

In most discussions of slavery, it is generally agreed that the life of domestic slaves was often far preferable to those working in the fields—whether in Charleston or the West Indies. Yet that could not be said for the unfortunate men, women, and children serving Caradeux's estate. The Comte, who often entertained lavishly, created singular parties that would long be remembered by his guests. One of the macabre party games by which he sought to achieve this distinction was to place a piece of fruit on a slave's head then invite his guests—both men and women, regardless of their experience—to shoot it off with either a pistol or an arrow at thirty paces. This and other spectacles, such as burying enslaved workers up to their necks and watching as biting flies feasted on their exposed heads, earned him the nickname "Caradeux the Cruel."[4] West Indian author, historian, and social theorist C. L. R. James (1901–1989) wrote that Caradeux "earned the admiration of his fellow slave owners for his vigor and ingenuity as a hanging propagandist,"[5] adding that once, following a mass execution, Caradeux nailed the heads of enslaved people to the palm trees decorously lining his plantation's hedges. His sexual abuse of the women he owned was legendary.

In this atmosphere of cruelty, Caradeux's aristocratic paradise was soon to crumble as the Slave Rebellion of 1791 began in Port-au-Prince. In August of that year, slaves from numerous plantations gathered one night at Bois Caiman (translated as "Alligator Forest") for a *vodou* ceremony. These common social gatherings of the island's enslaved were allowed by white planters, who felt the rituals promoted a more homogenous culture among the various African tribespeople.

There the celebrants slaughtered a pig, ceremoniously drank its blood, and vowed to overthrow the status quo. After dark on August 22, 1791, they began attacking planters and their families with the pruning hooks and machetes they used in the cane fields, sparing no one. They hacked planters to death in their beds, then raped their wives on top of the corpses. Some were crucified on the gates and walls of their own plantation houses. The rioters destroyed everything they could find connected to sugar cultivation—fields, mills, and warehouses. Anything that couldn't be burned was demolished with sledgehammers.

Upon hearing news of the uprising back at Port-au-Prince, Caradeux conscripted men from among his own and other urban slaves to form what he called the "Company of Africans" to push back the insurgents. The story of the Saint-Domingue Slave Revolt is a long and complex one of unimaginable brutality. Before it was over in 1804, an estimated two hundred thousand Black people had lost their lives, as had seventy-five thousand French and forty-five thousand British. Yet in the end, the formerly enslaved prevailed, accomplishing the only ultimately successful large-scale slave revolt in history.

Their victory sent shock waves around the world and certainly in Charleston, where rice and cotton planters already lived in constant fear of uprisings in an agricultural society where enslaved Black people greatly outnumbered their white overlords.[6]

Yet fear wasn't the only thing that emigrated from Saint-Domingue to Charleston as the rebellion occurred. Early in the conflict, Jean-Baptiste Caradeux, sensing the likelihood of the revolt's success, began sending valuables that were easy to ship and liquidate—silverware, coins, diamonds, and jewelry—to Charleston, as well as about twenty-four thousand dollars' worth of sugar. In 1792, Caradeux, his wife, young sons and daughter, his widowed sister, and about two dozen slaves quietly slipped out of one of Saint-Domingue's busy ports under cover of darkness and headed to Charleston to seek asylum.[7]

Caradeux, as well as many of his fellow Saint-Domingue refugees, undoubtedly chose Charleston as their new home because it, along with New Orleans, was a place not so very different from their island. As a leading port city, Charleston maintained a cosmopolitan air with close ties to Europe. And perhaps most importantly, Charleston's economy was likewise grounded in an agricultural society that exploited enslaved labor.[8]

With his comfortable nest egg awaiting him, Caradeux purchased a plantation in Berkeley County and established himself as a country planter. He also began a small, moderately successful brick and lumber business. He no longer entertained with lavish parties, nor did he participate in any way as a civic or military leader in the Lowcountry. The 1800 census indicated he had maintained a labor force of about twenty-five slaves, so he must not have had to sell any to support himself, but neither did he add any to replicate the great wealth and luxurious lifestyle he had enjoyed in Saint-Domingue. Instead, Jean-Baptist Caradeux spent the rest of his life in quiet comfort and obscurity as a country gentleman on his Lowcountry plantation. Though many in Charles Town knew of his past, few acknowledged or dwelt on it in polite society.

On May 25, 1810, Caradeux the Cruel died of natural causes on his Lowcountry plantation.

JOHN AND LAVINIA FISHER: THE TRUTH BEHIND THE LEGEND

F ew tourists leave Charleston without having heard some version of the macabre story of Lavinia Fisher, often reputed, incorrectly, to be the first female serial killer executed in the United States.[1] Like pirate Anne Bonny from an earlier chapter, most of what one hears about Lavinia is merely the stuff of ghost stories and legends, embellished with each retelling. Yet also like Bonny, even when you strip away the myths, Lavinia's scandalous life story has rightfully earned her a place among Charleston's most infamous characters, for she was indeed an unrepentant outlaw who lived a violent life in a place where women were better known for their graciousness and gentility.

No documentation gives insight to Lavinia's early years, but most sources put her birth around 1793. She married John Fisher and first entered the historical record when the young couple began managing two properties not far from Charleston (hence their names), the Five-Mile House and Six-Mile House, situated along the trading road that led to the Carolina "Backcountry" further inland.[2] Today we would recognize that trade route as Rivers Avenue and the tavern's site as near the Old Navy Hospital.

Contemporary reports confirm that the Fishers operated Six-Mile House as a tavern and inn, and probably Five-Mile House as a similar facility, though details of the latter are lacking in the historical record. Such establishments in the early 1800s were places where travelers could stop to water their horses, enjoy a meal and drink themselves, and perhaps rent a room for the evening before continuing on their way to the awaiting trade ships moored in Charleston Harbor. The transitory nature of such places sometimes lent themselves to other activities, such as gambling and prostitution, yet no evidence supports the claim that such was the case at either of the Fishers' properties.

Though rice cultivation and its supporting industries were the region's most impactful economic driver in the early nineteenth century, trading with Native Americans and the inland colonies was still a profitable business and an important part of Charleston's economy. Thus it was with a good deal of local concern when, in late 1818 and early 1819, this prosperous enterprise began being disrupted by a gang of highway robbers who would ambush traders along this well-traveled route. robbing them of their money, furs, deer skins, and other goods. Yet as the culprits were either well disguised or masked, no one had ever been able to identify the perpetrators.

Law enforcement officials began receiving reports that a number of traders who were believed to have sought lodging at or near the Fishers' taverns had never returned to Charleston with their pack trains and goods. An article in the *Charleston Courier* noted: "A gang of desperados have for some time past occupied certain houses in the vicinity of Ashley Ferry; practicing every deception upon the unwary and frequently committing robberies upon defenseless travelers."[3] Some in Charleston suspected that the Fishers might be among those involved "in the vicinity."

Here we'll pause for a moment to put aside some of the popular, but undocumented, myths about Lavinia Fisher. There is no evidence that she was a beautiful seductress who would lure travelers into drinking her drugged tea (or ale, depending on the storyteller's version), causing them to fall soundly asleep or pass out before either she or John stabbed them. She did not crush their skulls between her legs during sexual escapades, nor has there ever been any documentation that she lured them to bed, where, after they were asleep, John sprang a trap door that would tumble them down into a pit of sharpened spikes. No hundreds—not even dozens—of corpses were ever found at Six-Mile House or anywhere else on the Fishers' property. Indeed, an investigation at the time by local officials failed to turn up any evidence that would substantiate charges of murder against the couple.

When the officials' investigation failed to yield results, a vigilante group of Charlestonians took it upon themselves to ride out to the Fishers' taverns on Tuesday, February 16, 1819, to ascertain for themselves whether any suspected robbers were holed up there. Again according to the *Charleston Courier*: "As they could not be identified, and thereby brought to punishment, it was determined by a number of citizens to break them up, and they accordingly proceeded, in a cavalcade, on Thursday afternoon, . . . to proceed against the premises in such manner as circumstances might require."[4]

Sure enough, the citizens' cavalcade found a group they suspected of being involved in the robberies taking refuge at Five-Mile House, and they ordered the suspects out of the building before setting fire to it. As Five-Mile House burned to the ground, its smoke could be seen by those at Six-Mile House, who took the hint and escaped into the woods before the cavalcade's arrival. Again the vigilantes' search came up with no substantive evidence of misdeeds at this second location, but just to make sure things were on the level, one of their members, David Ross, stayed behind at Six-Mile House to keep an eye on things. This did not go well for Mr. Ross.

After the Charleston delegation had left, the robbers returned and brutally attacked Ross. As the men beat Ross nearly to death, according to his later testimony, he looked to Lavinia, hoping that as a woman she might plead mercy on his behalf. Rather than help him, however, Lavinia joined in the fray, choking Ross nearly to death with her bare hands before smashing his head through a window. Despite sustaining serious injuries, Ross escaped and returned to Charleston with his battered body and assailants' identifications as evidence of what had occurred.

About the same time, a traveler named John Peeples (or Peoples) was robbed and beaten along the road by the same gang; he too survived and returned to Charleston to share his story. Now, based on the statements and identifications provided by David Ross and John Peeples, officials again headed out to Six-Mile House on Saturday, February 20, arresting the Fishers and their business partner, William Hayward, along with several others.

The February 22 edition of the *Charleston Courier* related details of the arrests:

In Saturday's *Courier*, we gave some particulars of the conduct of a set of outlaws, who have for a long time past infested the road in the vicinity of this city, and whose outrageous conduct had of late become insupportable. We then stated that the occupants of a small house five miles from town, had been driven out, and the building burnt to the ground and that certain others, in possession of a house one mile above, had been compelled to leave it and another person [this would have been David Ross] put in possession of it by the owner [who would have been the Fishers' business partner]. It now appears, that as soon as the citizens had returned to town, the persons who had been thus compelled to leave the last-mentioned house, returned to it in the evening, and beat the person who had been put in possession in a most inhuman manner, when he escaped into the woods and made the best of his way to town. The next morning, the same gang stopped a traveler up the road, beat him cruelly, cut his head in several places, and then robbed him of about 30 or 40 in money [this would have been John Peeples]. These circumstances being made known to the civil authority, the Sheriff of this District collected a posse of citizens, and proceeded on Saturday afternoon to the spot, surrounded the house, and seized upon its occupants, (three men and two women) after which they burnt the house and outbuildings to the ground, without allowing the occupants to removed [sic] an article of its contents; brought the offenders to town, and committed them to jail. The posse found in an outhouse, the hide of a cow, which had been recently killed, and which was identified to be the property of one of our citizens. She had been missing for several days. This accounts for the manner in which the cows are disposed of which are so frequently stolen and never afterward heard of. The inmates of the house were armed with 10 or 12 muskets and a keg of powder, but the force which went against them was too imposing to admit of any chance of success in a resort to arms. One of the leaders in these high handed depredations was arrested into town on Saturday afternoon and likewise committed to jail. We trust that these decisive steps will restore quiet to the neighborhood, and enable our country brethren to enter and leave the city without the fear of insult or robbery.

The following is a correct list of the members of the gang who were apprehended and committed to prison on Saturday night. John Fisher, Lavinia Fisher, his wife, Wm. Heyward, James M'Elway, Jane Howard and Seth Young. It is supposed there are more of them lurking about and is hoped the vigilance of the police and citizens will ferret them out and bring them to justice.

We are informed and requested to state that Mr. John People, who was robbed and unmercifully beaten by the villains mentioned above, is an honest, industrious young man from the country, and had a sum of money entrusted to his care, which the robbers took from him.[5]

Though the Fishers were initially charged with "mayhem" (roughly equivalent to attempted murder today) in the assault of David Ross, that charge was later changed to highway robbery in the case of John Peeples. History enthusiasts have long debated why the charges were changed. While no documentation definitively clears up the mystery, some have suggested that highway robbery was considered by many to be a crime just as egregious as murder and more egregious than assault and battery. In addition, highway robbery was a capital offense, which lends plausibility to this supposition. Thus, to clarify the often-misrepresented historical record, neither John nor Lavinia Fisher was ever charged with murder, much less serial murder, as both David Ross and John Peeples survived their ordeals and no evidence was ever found at either of the taverns to substantiate such a charge (other than that of the cow whose hide they found).

At their arraignment, the Fishers pleaded not guilty yet were remanded to the Charleston District Jail until their trial in May 1819, where they were found guilty of highway robbery and sentenced to death. Their appeal of the ruling provided the couple with a reprieve until the next court session began in January 1820, and they were returned to the District Jail.[6]

On September 13, 1819, the Fishers nearly escaped from the District Jail by creating a rope out of strips of cloth. John went down first and had almost reached the ground when the rope broke, leaving Lavinia trapped on the jail's upper floors. Rather than leave his wife behind, John remained below Lavinia's window and was, of course, recaptured.

The Fishers' appeal on January 17, 1820, was unsuccessful and they were sentenced to be hanged February 4. Some in the community pleaded for mercy so that the couple might have more time to reconcile themselves to God and their destiny. Thus the executions were postponed until February 18, coincidentally the anniversary of when the citizens' posse first went out to accost them, leaving poor David Ross behind. According to news accounts, John did use the extended time of the execution to seek solace from the local Baptist minister, the Reverend Dr. Richard Furman. Lavinia did not.

Here again, we take a moment to address some of the myths regarding Lavinia's execution. Though it is often cited as a fact, it is highly unlikely that Lavinia wore her wedding dress to the scaffold. Many versions of the oral tradition claim that she did so in an effort to garner public sympathy and calls for the commutation of her sentence. Others ascribe the wedding gown story to a claim that because a woman was the property of her husband, she could not be executed, which would be tantamount to stealing another's property. Therefore John would have to be executed first, making Lavinia, briefly at least, a widow before she could be hanged. Adherents of this tale claim she wore a wedding dress hoping that, given her purported great beauty, as soon as John was hanged, some (ridiculously foolish) man in the crowd might rush up onto the gallows and marry her on the spot, thereby preventing her execution.

Neither story holds true, however. In the first place, brides did not get married wearing lacy white wedding gowns as we think of them today. Also, prisoners of the Charleston District Jail wore and, if called for, were executed in standard prison attire, usually a simple shift resembling an unbleached sack. In addition, the Fishers' executions were well covered in contemporary news reports, which did not mention anything unusual about her attire.

For a more accurate version of the story, we again turn to the *Charleston Courier* of February 19, 1820:

The execution of John and Lavinia Fisher, for Highway Robbery, took place yesterday, in the suburbs of the city, agreeably to their sentences. They were taken from the jail about a quarter before 1 o'clock, in a carriage in which, besides the prisoners was the Reverend Dr. Furman, and an officer of the police. They were guarded by the Sheriff of the District, with his assistants, and a small detachment of cavalry. Arrived at the fatal spot, some time was spent in conversation and prayer.—Fisher protested his innocence of the crime for which he was to die to the last, but admitted that he has lived a wicked and abandoned life. He met his fate with great firmness: and expressed his obligations to the new Sheriff for his kindness and humanity. His wife did not display so much of fortitude or resignation—She appeared to be impressed with a belief, to the last moment, that she would be pardoned. A little past 2 o'clock the husband and wife embraced each other upon the platform, for the last time in this world, when the fatal signal was given—the drop fell—and they were launched into eternity. She died without a struggle or a groan; but it was some minutes before he expired and ceased to struggle. After hanging the usual time, their bodies were taken down and conveyed to Potter's Field, where they were interred. The concourse that attended the execution was immense. May the awful example strike deep into their hearts; and may it have the effect intended, by deterring others from pursuing those vicious paths which ended in infamy and death.[7]

Though some tour guides claim that the Fishers were buried either in the churchyard of the Circular Congregational Church (which, because of its location, can conveniently be included on ghost tours after dark, per city tourism ordinances) or in the Unitarian Church (which everyone agrees is easily the creepiest-looking churchyard in town), the *Courier*'s account makes it clear that the couple's bodies were buried in "Potter's Field."[8] Two potter's fields were in use at the time, one at what is now St. Luke's Chapel, located on the campus of the Medical University of South Carolina, and

CHARLESTON.

SATURDAY MORNING, FEB. 19, 1820.

THE EXECUTION

Of JOHN and LAVINIA FISHER, for Highway Robbery, took place yesterday, in the suburbs of the city, agreeably to their sentence. They were taken from the jail about a quarter before 1 o'clock, in a carriage; in which, besides the prisoners, was the Rev. Dr. FURMAN, and and an officer of police. They were guarded by the Sheriff of the District, with his assistants, and a small detachment of cavalry. Arrived at the fatal spot, some time was spent in conversation and prayer.— FISHER protested his innocence of the crime for which he was to die to the last, but admitted that he had lived a wicked and abandoned life. He met his fate with great firmness; and expressed his obligations to the new Sheriff for his kindness and humanity. His wife did not display so much of fortitude or resignation— She appeared to be impressed with a belief, to the last moment, that she would be pardoned. A little past 2 o'clock the husband and wife embraced each other upon the platform, for the last time in this world, when the fatal signal was given—the drop fell—and they were launched into eternity. She died without a struggle or a groan; but it was some minutes before he expired and ceased to struggle. After hanging the usual time, their bodies were taken down and conveyed to Potter's Field, where they were interred.

The concourse that attended the execution was immense. May the awful example strike deep into their hearts; and may it have the effect intended, by deterring others from pursuing those vicious paths which end in infamy and death.

CONGRESS.—The Missouri Bill again came before

The account of the execution of John and Lavinia Fisher, *Charleston Courier*, February 19, 1820. *The (Charleston) Post and Courier Archives*

the other behind the Old District Jail. Having died not only poor but also a condemned criminal, it is likely that Lavinia's corpse, as well as John's, was interred behind the District Jail. Whether her ghost really haunts the old jail is anybody's guess.

DEATH OF THE
CAROLINA PARAKEET

N orth America's only native parrot was a colorful, vivacious bird with vibrant shades of green, a yellow head, and a reddish orange face. Once plentiful in Charleston's Lowcountry, the Carolina parakeet (*Conuropsis carolinensis*) nested in tree cavities of deciduous forests from the Gulf of Mexico to the Great Lakes and west to Nebraska. Local Native Americans called them *puzzi la nee*, "head of yellow."[1]

This 1825 painting of Carolina parakeets by noted ornithologist John J. Audubon was published in his book *Birds of America*. Native Americans in the region called them *puzzi la nee*, "head of yellow." *WikiMedia Commons*

Carolina parakeets lived off fruits, seeds, thistles, and cockleburs. Unfortunately, they also had a taste for cultivated crops such as corn, grain, and apples. Naturalist John J. Audubon noted that the Carolina parakeet "eats or destroys almost every kind of fruit indiscriminately, and on this account is always an unwelcome visiter [sic] to the planter, the farmer, or the gardener. The stacks of grain put up in the field are resorted to by flocks of these birds, which frequently cover them so entirely, that they present to the eye, the same effect as if a brilliantly coloured carpet had been thrown over them."[2]

As an agricultural pest, the birds were killed in huge numbers during the nineteenth century. This was an easier task than one might think, for Carolina parakeets were very social creatures, and when fired upon, as Audubon goes on to describe, "All the survivors rise, shriek, fly round about for a few minutes, and again alight on the very place of most imminent danger. The gun is kept at work; eight or ten, or even twenty, are killed at every discharge. The living birds, as if conscious of the death of their companions, sweep over their bodies, screaming as loud as ever, but still return to the stack to be shot at, until so few remain alive, that the farmer does not consider it worth his while to spend more of his ammunition."[3]

The Carolina parakeet faced other challenges as well. One was the deforestation of its habitat for agricultural fields. The second was its beauty; the parakeet's bright plumage was coveted both for ladies' hats and military decorations. Third, some ornithologists suggest, their extinction could have been associated with a disease common at the time among poultry.

By the beginning of the twentieth century, sightings of the bird were restricted to the swamps of central Florida. The last known specimen to exist in the wild was killed in 1904.[4]

One of the last Carolina parakeets raised in captivity was a cherished family pet named Doodles. After being rejected by his captive mother, Doodles was hand raised by Smithsonian scientist Dr. Paul Bartsch, who recalled: "He shared our meals, was well behaved, and stuck to his own plate almost always."[5] He also enjoyed a good snuggle and naps, either with Dr. Bartsch or with the family's pet squirrel. Doodles has been memorialized in a 1906 photo, comfortably nestled on the tie of a man identified only as Mr. Bryan, perhaps a family friend or associate of the Bartsches.

This rare photo is of one of the last Carolina parakeets known to exist in captivity. Named Doodles, he was owned by Smithsonian scientist Paul Bartsch, who kept him as a family pet, and was said to have reasonably refined table manners. *WikiMedia Commons*

The last captive Carolina parakeet, named Incas, died February 21, 1918, nearly a year after the death of his mate, Lady Jane, at the Cincinnati Zoo, in the same cage in which America's last passenger pigeon had passed away several years before. Reports of the parakeets' sightings continued until the late 1920s, but none of the reports were substantiated by specimens. In 1938 a group of ornithologists claimed to have seen a flock of parakeets in the northern swamps of Charleston County near the Santee River; however, this sighting was doubted by most other ornithologists, as again no specimens were collected. No other sightings have been reported, and in 1939 the American Ornithologists' Union declared the Carolina parakeet extinct.

Today the Charleston Museum has the largest collection of Carolina parakeet skins and skeletons, about 720, in the world.[6]

PART V
PLACES WITH A PAST

THE CHAPELS OF BERKELEY COUNTY: STORIES OF WORSHIP, WAR, BETRAYAL, AND FEAR

Lowcountry plantations were big. Really big. So big in fact that it could take the better part of a day to travel to a neighbor's house or a full day to get to Charles Town's shipping wharfs. For much of the colonial period, rivers—particularly the Ashley, Cooper, and Santee, along with their tributaries—were the fastest, most practical way to travel. Traveling by land, on the other hand, could be a challenge, especially within the Lowcountry's landscape, where water bodies are everywhere. Today we drive so conveniently over bridges large and small that we are rarely aware of the innumerable creeks, swamps, and wetlands we are speeding over.

For eighteenth-century settlers, however, making that same trip by horse, buggy, or foot was a long and arduous process that involved traveling extra distances to cross the waters at places that were passable. Ferries were often required to get from one shore to the other, and rarely did they run on time. Getting the entire family, including one's enslaved labor force, to church each Sunday, especially in bad weather, could be a monumental undertaking.

Charleston's planter class resolved this problem by creating what were known as chapels of ease. These small houses of worship were located more or less centrally near rural plantations and served the spiritual needs of several families in the area. Parish ministers would come by weekly to hold services, preach sermons, and visit the sick and infirm on a rotating schedule. Generally speaking, parishioners still had to travel to the official parish church to receive Holy Sacraments such as the Eucharist, baptism, matrimony, etc. Barring the need for such high rituals, however, these satellite chapels provided a much more convenient option for plantation families to worship.

Today the remains of these small, simple structures, remotely located far up along Charleston's rivers, tucked within overgrown thickets or hidden just beyond the highways' tree line, are some of the oldest and most beautiful historic gems of the Carolina Lowcountry. The stories of two of them, the St. James Goose Creek Chapel of Ease and Strawberry Chapel, as told through the lives of three generations of the Chicken family, provide an intriguing glimpse into the colonial history of this wild and storied place.

THE CAMP

Perhaps no other place in America tells a more complete or poignant story of our nation's history than a small, unpretentious spot of woodland tucked away between the banks of Chapel Creek and what we know today as "old" State Highway 52, about a mile or two beyond Strawberry station on the 52 Bypass. Although today's suburban commuters zip past it on their daily trips to the city's urban core, this spot was once a full day's walk north from the wharves of colonial Charles Town.[1]

The site has served as a footpath, trade route, campsite, fortress, chapel of ease, and Baptist church. Events here vividly illuminate the stories of Native Americans, early colonists, enslaved peoples, Revolutionary War Patriots, the Lowcountry's antebellum plantation society, and Civil War soldiers—all of whom once lived, worshipped, married, fought, and died here. Dramas of both good and evil emanate from this silent spot, though decades of neglect have allowed its stories to fade into obscurity.

Simple geography plays a huge role in shaping history. Long before Europe's first settlers arrived in the New World, small animals crossed what we now know as Chapel Creek through the shallow, marshy waters that run along the edge of this property. Predators came to track smaller prey along the path, and eventually Native Americans joined the hunt as well, here where crossing the creek was easiest. Then, from the earliest days of European settlement in Carolina, colonial adventurers followed the Native American footpath up the spine of the Charles Town peninsula, roughly along what we identify today first as downtown Charleston's boutique retail and restaurant mecca of King Street, then changing names to Rivers Avenue, and finally stretching out to become State Highway 52.

Along this path the Charles Town colonists pursued trade with tribes deep within the colony's still unexplored interior, the northwestern frontier of the late seventeenth and early eighteenth centuries. Pack animals carried imported manufactured items outbound and trudged back piled with deerskins and pelts bound for the port of Charles Town, then on to European markets far across the Atlantic, where these valuable commodities were much in demand.

Traders usually walked the route on foot, reserving their valuable pack animals for the heavy bundles of goods strapped across the equines' sturdy backs. Generally speaking, mules and donkeys could cover about twenty miles a day before they balked, ready for an evening's rest. Because of that, many traders making their way along the popular path stopped here by the shallow freshwater creek the evening before beginning the final twenty-two-mile leg of their journey to Charles Town the next morning. The site came to be known among traders and frontiersmen simply as "the Camp."

One of the traders who frequented the trail was an ambitious young man named George Chicken, who, along with his pack ponies, spent many a night at the campsite. With an entrepreneurial spirit and perhaps tired of the grueling and dangerous life of an Indian trader, Chicken imagined the possibilities of a new vocation as a planter and merchant. He successfully applied for a small grant of land along the creek on which to build a tavern that would accommodate weary traders. That initial land grant quickly grew to about 1,150 acres upon Chicken's marriage to his neighbor's widow, seventeen-year old Catherine Bellamy. The couple would rear five children at the camp, later dividing their time between there and their Charles Town house on Tradd Street.

By that time, the colony's lucrative trade *with* Native Americans had devolved into the even more lucrative trading *of* Native Americans. George Chicken himself owned thirty-nine enslaved people, nine of whom were indigenous tribespeople.[2]

Only in recent years have most professional guides begun offering visitors more realistic, complete interpretations of slavery. Yet in addition to the hundreds of thousands of enslaved Africans brought to America through the port of Charleston, there was also the Native American slave trade—a chapter of Charleston's history that few guides include in their interpretations. Though not the only colony involved in the commercialization of enslaved Native Americans, colonial Charlestonians were among its most egregious practitioners, exporting men, women, and children primarily to the West Indies, where they were put to backbreaking work on huge sugar plantations.

Scholars have suggested that between Charles Town's founding in 1670 through the outbreak of the Yamasee War in 1715, as many as fifty thousand Native Americans were captured and sold through the colony's port, many more souls than were imported from Africa during the same period.[3] For decades, tethered lines of enslaved Native people languished at Chicken's camp on the last night of their lives in their homeland, waiting for sunrise to begin the final leg of their dreaded journey to the waiting slave ships in Charles Town's harbor.

One has to look closely beyond the tree line along Old State Highway 52 to see the remains of what was once George Chicken's campsite, established near the spot where Chapel Creek shallows out. What was once a Native American and colonial trade route today is managed by a nonprofit group seeking to restore the St. James Goose Creek Chapel of Ease/ Bethlehem Baptist Church Historical Site. *Photo © Leigh Jones Handal*

THE YAMASEE WAR

While the sordid slave trading enterprise returned fortunes for Charles Town's traders and merchants, it also forged more than a dozen of the region's indigenous tribes into a confederacy collectively known as the Yamasee (or Yemassee). The tribes were already angry about settlers' increasing encroachment on their lands, dwindling deer populations, unfair trade practices that left many in debt to the white man, and broken promises made by colonial fur traders. In an effort to resolve the conflict, the Commission on Indian Affairs sent a delegation to meet with the Yamasee at a small crossroads south of Charles Town along the Pocotaligo River on Maundy Thursday, April 14, 1715. There the commission's six-man delegation again promised to redress the Natives' grievances and went to bed satisfied that the matter was settled.

The Yamasee, however, had tired of promises. After debating among themselves throughout most of the night, they donned war paint before dawn the next morning and, shortly before the sun rose on Good Friday, brutally attacked the commission's delegation. Only two men escaped, injured but alive. Thomas Nairne, a Scots trader and the colony's first Indian agent—best known for documenting many of the Native Americans' lives and customs—was ritually tortured to death by fire over the course of the next three days. Some accounts describe Nairne's torture as his being "roasted alive" over an open flame. A traveling trader coming upon the site lay hidden in a nearby thicket, witnessing Nairne's agony yet unable to do anything to help.[4] It was the beginning of the most deadly Native American war in South Carolina's history.

The next day, the Yamasee broke into two groups. One headed to Port Royal, another small settlement south of Charles Town. One of the commission's delegates who had escaped made his way to a nearby plantation in time to send a messenger to warn the port's colonists of the rampage headed their way, allowing most to flee in time to escape death. Many of them headed out to sea on a recently captured smuggler's ship that was moored in the harbor. The second war party burned and plundered its way through St. Bartholomew's parish, between the Edisto and Combahee Rivers, killing more than one hundred colonists and enslaved workers within their path.

Charles Town's proprietary governor, Charles Craven, responded to these Yamasee atrocities by developing a plan that would mobilize the colony's forces under the command of Capt. Thomas Barker, a "brave young gentleman," according to letters written by the Reverend Francis LeJau.[5] LeJau (also spelled Le Jau) served the St. James Goose Creek Parish as one of the first missionaries sent to the Carolina colony by the Society for the Propagation of the Gospel in Foreign Parts (SPGFP) to save the imperiled souls of the heathen Natives and African slaves living within the colony. Upon his arrival, however, a number of Charlestonians suggested that the souls of a number of good English Anglicans within his parish outpost could use a bit of "polishing up" as well. Thus LeJau set about ministering to all in his parish—Black, white, and red skinned. A French Huguenot who converted to the Anglican faith after King Louis XIV revoked the Edict of Nantes in 1685, LeJau regularly sent reports to his SPGFP sponsors in England, chronicling not only the Yamasee War but also much of what we know today about this period of Charles Town's colonial history.

Governor Craven's plan called for Captain Barker to not only mobilize a professional, paid army but also to raise and direct about sixteen militia groups, volunteers acting under the orders of local leaders. George Chicken was one of these local "colonels" and quickly organized his neighbors into a volunteer fighting force. Under Captain Barker's leadership, these groups immediately set about establishing forts to create a thirty-mile safety perimeter around Charles Town. As the volunteers—colonists of European descent as well as enslaved Africans who were trusted to bear military arms—took up their defensive positions, most of the women, children, and infirm fled to Charles Town to seek safety within its protective walls. One family, the Hernes, did not.

Within days, Yamasee confederates crossed the Santee River north of Charles Town, coming upon John Herne's plantation. Having successfully lived among and traded with Native Americans for many years, Herne (sometimes spelled Hyrne) was no stranger to the life and challenges of the Carolina frontier. He and his large family had ignored the governor's warnings for those in outlying areas to evacuate to Charles Town, instead trusting that his long-standing ties with local Natives would protect his interests.

Therefore, he was not surprised when a small group of warriors approached his house in a relaxed, friendly manner, asking if he might share his evening's meal with them, which he did. Herne's hospitality was sorely repaid, however, when after dinner the Natives bludgeoned him to death before signaling their compatriots, hidden in the woods, to attack and kill the rest of his family and his enslaved laborers.[6] Little did Herne suspect that his death would be responsible for many others, at least in part because of an old grudge held by a freedman he had left to die in the woods years before.

According to LeJau's letters, upon hearing of Herne's death, Captain Barker led a hundred or so men, many of whom were among the missionary's own parishioners, out to meet the Yamasee near the Santee River site of the Herne family's massacre. Their route had been laid out by a trusted freedman named Wateree Jack.

THE BETRAYAL OF WATEREE JACK

Jack was a Native American of the Wateree tribe who was found orphaned when just a young child in the aftermath of a North Carolina tribal skirmish in the mid-1690s.[7] Taken captive and enslaved, he grew up at Boochawee Hall plantation, the country seat of James Moore I, located not far from George Chicken's camp. Moore, an Irish immigrant to Charles Town by way of Barbados, was an industrious, ruthless, and driven man who muscled his way into becoming the colony's proprietary governor from 1700 to 1703. After his term in office, he led several raids on Spanish missions in Florida, where he amassed a fortune by capturing hundreds of Native Americans whom he sold into slavery. By virtue of his daughter Rebecca's marriage, Moore was also the father-in-law of Capt. Thomas Barker.

At that time, it was common for Carolina's frontier families to "keep an Indian" among their workers. Unlike most field slaves, these trusted servants were allowed a bit of autonomy, often coming and going as they pleased, sometimes for extended periods, to hunt turkey, deer, rabbits, and other game for the settlers' tables.[8] Jack, a skilled woodsman who knew virtually every nuance of Charles Town's frontier landscape, hunted game for the Moore family, as well as serving as a scout and Native American translator.

After years of exemplary service and behavior, Wateree Jack had become so trusted by the Moores that in 1697 he was given the task of traveling to Virginia with £100 (pounds sterling), a small fortune, to buy additional ponies for the family's growing pack trading enterprise. Traveling with Jack were the aforementioned John Herne and a man named Robert Stevens, both of whom felt "safe by the assistance of Indian Jack their Guide and Interpreter."[9]

Despite Jack's best scouting efforts, the trio was brutally attacked one evening by a group of local Natives as they slept along the trade route in the upper part of North Carolina. Awakening to the noise of the attack, John Herne fled, swimming across a nearby river to safety and leaving Jack, Stevens, and the money behind. Stevens was horribly bludgeoned to death, "his head bruised all to pieces."[10] Jack was critically wounded by a gunshot to his upper leg.

While the Natives were distracted with plundering the campsite, Jack managed to slip away into the woods, hoping Herne would return to help him. When Herne never came, Jack began to stumble through the woods, fighting for his life as the wound in his leg bled and throbbed with each step, barely surviving by eating whatever berries and plants he could find. For eleven days he limped northward before finally reaching the homestead of a charitable family in Virginia, who took him in and found him the skilled medical attention he needed to survive his wound.

As Jack painfully made his way through the forest, John Herne returned to the site of the attack, hoping to recover the £100. He found only a few pieces of silver that had been dropped by the marauders, as well as the three horses that had been left behind grazing. Putting rocks into the pockets of Robert Stevens's corpse, Herne sank the body into the river, as respectful a burial as he felt he could manage at the time.

Months passed before Wateree Jack was healthy enough to travel again. As soon as he was able, however, he signed on with a group of traders heading south so that he could return home to his master at Boochawee Hall. Jack was an appreciated addition to the pack train, serving as both scout and interpreter on the way back to Charles Town. They finished the 941-mile journey in thirty-seven days, arriving at Boochawee on September 15, 1697.

Sometime around 1701, James Moore I manumitted his trusted servant, giving him the title "Indian Warr [sic] Captain"[11] and his own horse. As a free man now, Jack shared in the profits that came with Moore's trading enterprises, both of pelts and humans, and soon became comfortably wealthy himself.

Still, in one sense, not much seemed to change in Wateree Jack's life. He continued working for the Moores—both James Moore I, who died in 1706, then for his son, James Moore II. Because of his position of trust and leadership along the frontier, Wateree Jack was present as Captain Barker, James Moore II, George Chicken, and others discussed military tactics against the Yamasee along Charles Town's northern front, near John Hernes's homestead.

Yet in another sense, something very much had changed in Jack after the traumatic attack along the trading path to Virginia. Goose Creek historian Dr. Michael Heitzler believes that Jack developed a "conflicted conviction and recall of boyhood promises, and tribal allegiances haunted him"[12] as he reflected upon the countless Natives whose enslavement had made the Moores a wealthy family.

And he never forgot that John Herne had abandoned him, leaving him to die, along the road to Virginia.

One must wonder if these thoughts were in Jack's mind as the freedman clandestinely sent a messenger early the next morning to the Yamasee gathered along the shores of the Santee River, revealing details of the colonists' strategies. Three days after the Herne family's massacre, the Yamasee confederates, with Wateree Jack among them, lay in ambush, awaiting Captain Barker and his men on their way to the Herne homestead.

The ambush was easy to devise, as two years earlier, on September 5, 1713, a "great hurricane" had roared its way ashore near the property that lay between Herne's farm and Charles Town.[13] Captain Barker had not visited the site near Eutaw Springs, later known as Barker's Savannah, since the storm, and therefore he was not familiar with the devastated landscape. It was littered with forest debris and huge, twisted trees toppled over, their massive root systems ripping up large chunks of the surrounding ground as they came crashing down. The damage had been extensive, providing plenty of spaces to hide.

As the colonial force came within sight, Wateree Jack fired the first shot, instantly killing Captain Barker, who fell from his horse. That shot was immediately followed by a large volley of shots coming from behind uprooted tree trunks and fallen branches on all sides. Before the colonial force had time to realize what was happening, arrows, tomahawks, and hatchets flew from every direction. Within scant minutes, a third of Barker's troops lay dead, according to accounts provided by the Reverend LeJau, who noted that ten of his own parishioners were among those left lying lifeless on the forest's floor. The rest fled, some back to Chicken's camp.

After the Eutaw Creek ambush, Wateree Jack disappears from the Reverend LeJau's reports to the SPGFP, and thus from the historical record. His fate will undoubtedly remain unknown. A year after the war, however, the Colonial Assembly confirmed that Wateree Jack was the "author of most of ye mischief they have done to us."[14]

In subsequent letters, LeJau related that the Yamasee next attacked a makeshift fort at Benjamin Schenkingh's plantation, which was defended by about thirty white and Black settlers. According to LeJau's reports, the Natives asked for and were granted a truce.[15] Upon entering the fortification, however, the Yamasee killed more than half the colonists.

The war continued to fare badly for the sparsely populated colonists, the Yamasee picking off each family's settlement as they made their way ever closer toward Charles Town, where they planned to brutally push the English back into the sea from which they had come. With twelve hundred colonists defending their homes against ten thousand Yamasee confederates, historians agree that at this point, the very survival of Charles Town as a English colony was seriously in question.

RETURN TO CHICKEN'S CAMP

By this time, those who could had abandoned their homesteads and fled to Charles Town, seeking protection. In his letters, the Reverend LeJau recounts seeing first this frontier family, then that one, and finally his own wife and daughters, flee past his parsonage door near the Goose Creek bridge on their way to Charles Town. With the swelling refugee population and transportation routes disrupted, residents and refugees alike soon faced the pangs of starvation and lack of many supplies. Those within the colony's walls were beginning to panic.

Isolated settlers who couldn't make it to Charles Town fled for cover to Mulberry Castle, a strong brick plantation house set on a high bluff just up the road from Chicken's camp. Built c. 1714 over a fortified cellar, the house had firing slits in the foundation walls and four defensive corner pavilions, each with windows on three sides, providing a wide range of aim. Judiciously bypassing this well-fortified house, the Yamasee continued to pick off homesteaders one by one before reaching Chicken's camp. Presumably this would be their last stop before attacking Charles Town the next morning. They were in for a bit of a surprise.

Mulberry Castle, c. 1714, was built shortly before the start of the Yamasee War. Its sturdy brick construction and corner pavilions served as a safe shelter for isolated colonists in the path of the Yamasee warriors. *WikiMedia Commons*

George Chicken, assuming the rank of colonel, had formed a volunteer citizens' militia comprising about seventy of his neighbors and set out to stop the Yamasees' progress. Before leaving the camp, however, Chicken had used his years of experience fighting in Queen Anne's War (1706) and against the Tuscarora in North Carolina several years earlier to build a palisade wall with crude ramparts around his little trading camp. Correctly guessing that the Yamasee would try to cross the creek at the camp, Chicken's goal was to use the fortress to delay the Native war party. Under his direction, both Black and white colonists quickly cleared trees to create an open firing zone, using the fallen logs to build a formidably high rampart from which they could shoot down. Chicken then briefed his enslaved workers, as well as those of his neighbors, along with the remaining women and children, on how to use the bulwark to their advantage should the Yamasee come.

On May 8, LeJau traveled from his parsonage to the refugees at Chicken's camp, bringing news of the war along with his sermon. With the men of Chicken's militia fighting further inland, LeJau found "the greatest Part of their Women & Children . . . in Town."[16] Some of the survivors of Wateree Jack's deadly ambush days before had also taken refuge here and were ready to lend a hand. LeJau reported: "'Every family had fled to town, except in one place,' at the camp, where reinforced with Captain Barker's ambush survivors, 'seventy white men and forty Negroes had surrounded themselves with a breast-work, and resolved to remain and defend themselves in the best manner they could.'"[17]

Though scant details of the skirmish have survived, on June 11, 1715, this mixed group of Barker's ambush survivors, women, and the enslaved, by sheer effort, guts, or prayer, somehow stopped the Natives from crossing the creek. The Yamasee turned back. It was a fatal mistake—after a day of rest, on June 13, the repelled Natives walked directly into an ambush set by Chicken's men and were routed, effectively ending the colony's most threatening confrontation with America's indigenous people.

Though some of the Yamasee sued for peace, others fled to Spanish Florida, where they joined runaway slaves and others to form tribes collectively known as the Seminole, a name derived from the Spanish word *cimarrón*, meaning "wild runaways."[18]

Today scholars recognize the Yamasee War as one of the most disruptive conflicts of colonial America, as for more than a year, the Charles Town colony faced the real possibility of annihilation. Nearly 7 percent of South Carolina's settlers died fighting the Yamasee, making it one of the bloodiest wars in American history.[19]

ST. JAMES GOOSE CREEK CHAPEL OF EASE

After the harrowing conflict known as the Yamasee War, George Chicken declared the site of the camp where Barker's ambush survivors, enslaved workers, and a handful of women miraculously turned back the Yamasee to be "sacred ground," as it held the blood, and probably the earthly remains, of those who fought atop the camp's hastily constructed palisade walls and arguably saved the Charles Town colony from destruction. Chicken donated the campsite to the St. James Goose Creek Parish, which built an antebellum chapel of ease here, as it was convenient to several nearby plantation families and was situated on high ground next to a reliable freshwater spring. Masons, many of whom were probably enslaved, built the small, traditionally designed cruciform house of worship out of locally made bricks.

Colonel Chicken continued to serve as a colonial leader for another decade, and on March 10, 1725, responded "Present" when roll call was taken at the Second Royal Assembly, in which he served as a representative. Afterward he returned to his town house on Tradd Street, where he died two days later. Though no cause of death was recorded, Charles Town was experiencing one of its periodic yellow fever epidemics, which has led some to speculate this may have been the cause. His son, George Chicken Jr., led the funeral procession from downtown to the little chapel by Church Creek, where he and his family buried their patriarch.[20]

On June 13, 1725, three months after Colonel Chicken's death and ten years after the defeat of the Yamasee, the Reverend Richard Ludlam led the chapel's parishioners in their first celebration of Mass at the St. James Goose Creek Chapel of Ease. Regular services continued here through the late 1760s or early 1770s, as tensions began to rise in the years leading up to the American Revolution.

As the inevitability of a split with Britain approached, an increasing number of Carolinians began to shun all things British, including Anglicanism. By the time the American Revolution was won, the chapel's beams had begun to bow ominously under the weight of its deteriorating roof. Archaeological evidence suggests that the chapel may have burned around this time, the flame perhaps sparked by the British.

Because the economic interests of many of Charles Town's planters and merchants were closely tied to Great Britain, the American Revolution could almost be viewed as a civil war here, the conflict often pitting brother against brother in its early days. Despite the divided loyalties, even among families, Patriots and Loyalists alike continued to inter their loved ones in the shade of the ancient forest surrounding the crumbling chapel. Even though its churchyard remained in use, the fading popularity of Anglicanism immediately before and after the Revolution sealed the fate of the little chapel, and it was never again used actively by an Episcopal congregation.

Instead it moldered in the sullen forest until a group of energetic Baptists breathed new life into George Chicken's storied campsite. The Reverend Matthew McCullers visited the chapel, by then recognizable only as a pile of mostly broken bricks, where he prayed with eight "brethren" on June 13, 1812, ninety-seven years after the Yamasee defeat, and proclaimed the founding of the new Bethlehem Baptist Church.

Gathering some of the chapel's scattered bricks to build a new foundation and steps, congregation members hammered together a twenty- by thirty-foot clapboard church near where the Anglican chapel had stood. Once again, congregants filled the quiet countryside with soul-lifting hymns, proclaimed the Holy Gospel, baptized new members, married hopeful couples, and expanded the churchyard with new interments. In concert with the St. James Goose Creek Parish vestry, they also established a school and hired a teacher to educate the poor, even as the drumbeat to the next great war hastened, when Union soldiers would become the next military force to march past its doors.

After the Civil War, the population center for the Goose Creek parish changed. Travelers no longer moved around by traversing local rivers via ferries but instead traveled more readily by better maintained roads and trains. As the area's population recentered itself around the new railroad depots, so did Bethlehem Baptist Church. Its congregation abandoned their rural, plantation-era graveyard by the Chapel Creek shallows. Congregants disassembled the wooden church, hauled it by sections on carts four and a half miles northwest, rebuilt it with new doors and window sashes, and renamed it Groomsville Baptist Church. The renovation infused new energy into the little congregation, but it once again consigned the old chapel of ease churchyard to the mercy of the elements.

As the decades of the twentieth century rolled by, the forest once again reclaimed the plat of land that had been the site of George Chicken's camp. Tree roots dislodged headstones, which often shattered as they fell. Vines and vegetation engulfed Revolutionary-era box tombs, hastening the inevitable crumbling and disintegration of the bricks' mortar. Demarcations denoting most of those interred in Chicken's "sacred ground" were lost altogether.

Groomsville Baptist Church still stands today but is no longer in use. Descendants of the same families who lie buried at Chicken's campsite are buried here today. *Photo © Leigh Jones Handal*

118

The headstone of Eliza Donnely (c. 1808–1858) lay broken and covered up by leaves and soil for decades as the former churchyard was consumed by the elements after 1938, when the last internment occurred here. Today Mrs. Donnely's headstone has been restored and reset. *Photo © Leigh Jones Handal*

Yet a few members of local families with relatives interred there remembered visiting the abandoned churchyard and the stories of those who reposed here, stories passed down to them by their grandparents. These families brought the site to the attention of Goose Creek mayor and local historian Dr. Michael Heitzler, who worked with the Berkeley County Chamber of Commerce to form a nonprofit in 2014, the St. James Goose Creek Chapel of Ease/Bethlehem Baptist Church Historical Site, whose mission is to protect and preserve the site of Chicken's old camp and those whose remains repose here in the woods. It was rededicated as "sacred ground" on June 13, 2015, three centuries to the day after the last significant battle of the Yamasee War. Research, cleanup, and interpretation of the graves tell the stories of those buried there, stories that in turn interpret the history of America from Charles Town's earliest colonial days through the first third of the twentieth century. The following are just a few examples of those stories rediscovered to date, stories of people whose names have never made it into the history books, but who each contributed to our community's timeline in significant ways of their own.

DR. ROBERT BROUN (1715–NOVEMBER 23, 1757) AND ELIZABETH THOMAS BROUN (1722–JUNE 6, 1766)

Mary Broun Loocock laid this box tomb monument to honor her parents, Elizabeth and Robert Broun (also spelled Brown). Robert Broun was born the year the Yamasee were turned back at Chicken's camp. Broun, a twenty-one-year-old physician, emigrated from Scotland with his parents. It is not known where Dr. Broun received his medical degree at such a young age; however, he was readily welcomed into the homes of the area's most prominent families, leaving one to assume that he was well educated and competent.[21] Though his parents continued on to settle in Virginia, Dr. Broun remained here, married Elizabeth Thomas, and established Brounfield Plantation on the headwaters of Foster Creek.[22]

AARON LOOCOCK (1733–FEBRUARY 10, 1794)

English immigrant Aaron Loocock began his rise to local prominence by trading furs and slaves before becoming a planter. Upon his marriage to Mary Broun, daughter of Dr. and Mrs. Robert Broun (above), he acquired Brounfield Plantation. While many Charles Town planters made fortunes cultivating indigo, the source of a rich blue dye so highly valued that England placed a bounty on its import, Loocock experimented with growing madder, a plant used to make a red dye. Although he never achieved the success of indigo, Loocock's book, *Some Observations and Directions for the Culture of Madder*, was published in 1775 by Peter Timothy, who also published the Declaration of Independence locally, was editor of the *South-Carolina*

Gazette, and was the son of Elizabeth Timothy, the first female publisher in America.

When Charles Town fell to British forces in 1780, Loocock avoided being imprisoned and having his lands confiscated by taking an oath to not take up arms again against the British. Upon the Patriots' victory, however, many of the British oath takers, including Loocock, had their lands confiscated by the American victors. Detained in the Provost's Dungeon under Charles Town's Old Exchange Building, Loocock fought back: "During the 1783 session of the House of Representatives, William Clarkson petitioned on behalf of Goose Creeker, Aaron Loocock. He asked for relief from the Confiscation Act, citing Loocock's aid to prisoners of war in England and asking that his property and citizenship be returned to him."[23] It was.

In 1790, having added more properties to his portfolio, Loocock was elected a representative to the convention that adopted South Carolina's first constitution. He was then elected to represent the St. James Goose Creek Parish in the new state's first House of Representatives. He declined to serve, however, on January 25, 1791, claiming that he was dedicating most of his time to caring for his profitable mercantile business in Charles Town.[24]

CAPT. ARCHIBALD BROUN
(JANUARY 9, 1752–DECEMBER 11, 1797)

Archibald Broun's box tomb was erected by his son, Robert Broun (1781–1809, not to be confused with Dr. Robert Broun, Archibald's father). A committed American Patriot from the beginning of the revolutionary conflict, Archibald Broun traveled to France shortly before the Revolutionary War to negotiate a loan for military supplies and equipment. There he met and befriended the famed Marquis de Lafayette. Though Broun was successful in his ambassador's mission, his returning ship, which was carrying the arms and supplies he had secured from France, was captured by the British. Though no documentation relates whether Broun was also captured at the time, if he was he must have escaped, as his story picks up shortly thereafter in Boston, from whence he galloped posthaste back to Goose Creek and fought for Americans' liberty as an infantry captain.

Captain Broun's streak of bad luck continued, however. One night, as he was serving at the Siege of Savannah, he arose and quietly walked to the perimeter of his camp (undoubtedly to answer the call of nature). In a most unfortunate accident, he stumbled upon one of his own sentries, who had drifted off to sleep. Suddenly awakened, the panicked sentry mistakenly stabbed and severely wounded Broun with his bayonet.

Broun returned home to Brounfield to recuperate, where on August 17, 1780, he married Mary Deas, daughter of his wealthy neighbors, John and Elizabeth Allen Deas of Thoroughgood Plantation. With the wealth that Mary brought to the match, Archibald acquired more plantations and was listed as among the five wealthiest landholders in the parish.[25] When his old friend the Marquis de Lafayette returned to visit Charleston after the Revolution, Captain Broun entertained him at a grand dinner held in his honor at his Blessing Plantation.

Broun never fully recovered from his war wound, which troubled him for the rest of his life. After twenty years, complications associated with his wound finally led to his death. Brounfield Plantation then passed to Archibald's sister, Mary, who married Aaron Loocock.

L. E. A. SHIER (SEPTEMBER 28, 1854–SEPTEMBER 10, 1859)

Perhaps one of the most poignant stories to be found in the former Bethlehem Baptist churchyard is that of Miss L. E. A. Shier, whose Christian names have been lost to history, yet whose story seemed especially salient as the COVID-19 pandemic arrived in 2020. Miss Shier was not yet five years old in 1859 when the Lowcountry was ravaged by one of its frequent epidemic waves, this time with what locals called "the bilious fever," the same year Charleston was ravished by a yellow fever epidemic. Though her physician did all he could for her, the little girl died less than a week after developing symptoms of a high fever, nausea, and dehydration. The Shiers had a distinctive headstone carved for her featuring a trillium flower, a three-leaf perennial that blooms abundantly around her grave early each spring, giving rise to her popular nickname, "the Trillium Angel."

THE LOST VILLAGE OF CHILDSBURY

Few traces of Charles Town's first planned inland settlement remain, although archaeologists and scuba divers occasionally pull up artifacts recalling James Child's great, failed civic endeavor.[26] An early settler, Child was granted twelve hundred acres known as Strawberry along the West Branch of the Cooper River in 1698, where he established a ferry at the spot where the river became too shallow for larger, oceangoing ships to continue upriver.

Yet Child had bigger ambitions than building just a ferry landing. Over the next decade, he added fifteen hundred acres in land grants to his property holdings, and by 1707 he had published plans for the first inland satellite colony of Charles Town. Naming the new village Childsbury (also spelled Childbury) after himself, the village featured 182 residential lots laid out in traditional squares and streets that were an amazing sixty-six feet wide, plenty of room for carriages to pass alongside each other without incident. He also set aside six hundred acres for a communal farm and another one

Image of rural families leaving Strawberry Ferry Landing to attend church in downtown Charleston circa the 1890s. *South Caroliniana Library*

hundred acres on a high bluff on which to build a fort that could protect villagers from unfriendly Native Americans, the St. Augustine Spanish, or even pirates. By the time James Child died, around 1720, he had already sold many of the lots, and plans for the village's principal civic buildings were well under way.

Strawberry Chapel, established as a chapel of ease for St. John's Berkeley Parish Church (also known as Biggins Church) located ten miles away, was completed by 1725. Unlike other chapels of ease, an act of the Colonial Assembly passed on December 9, 1725, allowed Strawberry to perform the rites for baptisms and burials. Though no documentation exists, this might have been due to the influence of the powerful Ball family of Comingtee Plantation. A small yet finely built brick structure covered in scored stucco (very fashionable for the period), it featured a jerkin-head roof, a more sophisticated combination of the common gable and hip roof styles. Its principal south facade had double three-paneled doors with an overhead fan light and shuttered windows on either side. Both the eastern and western facades' single doors featured decorative rosette windows above and were each flanked by a pair of windows. Its northern facade included a small enclosed vestry.

Space was also set aside in the village plan for a tavern, a racetrack, and workshops for a tanner, butcher, shoemaker, and carpenters. The Commons House of Assembly established market days in the village on Tuesdays and Saturdays, along with annual fairs in May and October. A "free school" was completed by 1733 and a French Huguenot couple named Dutarque were hired as its teachers, fitting the qualifications as prescribed by law: "That the Master shall be of the religion of the Church of England and conform to the same, and shall be capable to teach the learned languages—that is to say, the Latine (sic) and Greek tongues—and also the useful part of the Mathematicks, and to catechize and instruct the youth in the principles of the Christian religion as professed in the Church of England."[27]

By the late 1730s, however, Charles Town's economic base had shifted from trade with Native Americans to the development of its antebellum plantation society. Plantations, by definition self-sustaining, usually had their own riverside docks, eliminating the need for a central shipping point such as Strawberry Ferry. Skilled enslaved laborers on the plantations supplanted the need for Childsbury's artisans. Small farmers and tradesmen could not compete with the sprawling estates, and by 1750, Childsbury began to be gradually absorbed into nearby plantations. The village tavern remained active for a couple more decades; semiannual fairs and horse races continued through the mid-1700s as well. Though Strawberry Chapel continued to nurture its congregation through the nineteenth century, by the time of the American Revolution, Childsbury essentially no longer existed.

The only visible remains of the village today is Strawberry Chapel, which is privately owned and not open to the public, though services are held there several times a year. The village's high bluff is a state heritage preserve, rarely visited except by ardent anglers and a few archaeologists.

All that remains today of Childsbury is its beautiful Strawberry Chapel (c. 1725). *Library of Congress*

THE HARSH EDUCATION OF LITTLE MISS CHICKEN

Around 1748, in the waning yet still optimistic days of Childsbury's existence, a French Huguenot couple named Monsieur and Madame Dutarque ran a small school in the little village on the western branch of the Cooper River. One of their two boarding students at the time was a young girl named Catherine Chicken, who was about seven years old.

Though she was too young to appreciate her social status at the time, Catherine was related to two—and now even three—very influential Charles Town families. On her mother's side, she was the great-granddaughter of James Child, the founder of Childsbury. Catherine's mother, Lydia, had inherited her grandfather's Strawberry Plantation, as well as the Strawberry Ferry, which provided villagers with direct access to the main trading route to Charles Town.

On her father's side, Catherine was the granddaughter of none other than the legendary Col. George Chicken, who had led the final, decisive charge against the Yamasee in 1715 and was widely credited with saving the colony of Charles Town from destruction. In fact, Catherine had been named for her paternal grandmother, Catherine Bellamy Chicken.

Catherine's father, Capt. George Chicken, had also earned a reputation in his own right as someone who often fought Native Americans, having led Carolina's troops against the Cherokee of western North Carolina. Also like his father, Captain Chicken had distinguished himself as a civic leader within the Charles Town colony, holding numerous offices and appointments and becoming a successful planter, trader, and large landholder. Following the death of his first wife, Captain Chicken married Lydia Turnsteed Child of Childsbury. Catherine was their only child—her father died in March 1745 at the age of thirty-six, while Catherine was still a toddler. Captain Chicken left most of his estate to his son and daughter by his first marriage, noting in his will that he knew his beloved little Catherine would be well taken care of by virtue of her mother's family's wealth.

Nevertheless, life could be precarious for young widows in those days, and less than two years later, Lydia Turnsteed Child Chicken remarried, this time to Elias Ball II, who had inherited nearby Comingtee Plantation, located just a mile or so from Childsbury where the Cooper River branched into its east and west tributaries. Ball had recently added Kensington Plantation to his landholdings, and by virtue of his marriage to Lydia, he added Strawberry Plantation as well, creating a huge plantation empire. Soon the Balls were expecting their first child together and thought it best to temporarily board Catherine with her Childsbury school master and his wife until after the new baby arrived and Lydia had regained her strength following the birth.

This much of Catherine Chicken's story, then, is indeed a "veritable happening of colonial Carolina,"[28] as her life, including her later married life as Catherine Chicken Simons, mistress of Middleburg Plantation, is well documented. Indeed, to this day, her oil portrait remains a cherished family heirloom, one which distinctly shows a slight drooping weakness on the left side of her face.

The rest of Catherine's story, however, has come down to us primarily as an oral history, with myriad versions of the exact details. With that caveat in mind, what follows is an explanation of what happened one night in the graveyard of her great-grandfather's Strawberry Chapel.

Given the prominence and wealth of Catherine's families, one might assume that the Dutarques would feel honored to be entrusted with her as a boarder at their little school. Perhaps. Yet if so, that privilege must also have come with a great sense of responsibility, and perhaps a touch of anxiousness, for the child's welfare and safety. Nevertheless, all oral histories of Miss Chicken's story agree that the Dutarques were a stern couple who brooked no misbehavior from their students.

A much beloved—and admittedly somewhat spoiled—child, Catherine was unhappy being with the Dutarques from the start. Although her cousins attended school there as well, she was the only one in her family who had to board there, and to her it just didn't seem fair, "for little Catherine had been always treated like a princess, and had thought the world was but a pretty place made for her to play in. Now she found it a bigger and sadder place than she had fancied."[29]

On an unseasonably hot day in May 1748, both of the Dutarques, as well as Catherine, were feeling a bit irritable and out of sorts, according to Mrs. Arthur Gordon Rose's account, written in 1913 for the Colonial

Dames of South Carolina and declared by many to be "from all appearances the most accurate and accepted" version of the story.[30] Catherine was not focused on her assignment that beautiful spring day and was anxious to be outside playing. Madame Dutarque accused her of being lazy and set as her punishment "the sewing of a long seam." Madame's angry outburst caused Monsieur Dutarque to rebuke his wife, reminding her of the possibility that Catherine might complain about them to her mother and stepfather, which wouldn't be good. Rather than continue to escalate the argument, Madame Dutarque decided it would be best to take this opportunity to walk to the nearby market square and allow everyone's tempers to cool a bit before that evening's supper.

Monsieur Dutarque went back to his reading, and for a while Catherine tried to focus on completing the long seam she had been assigned as a punishment for her inattentiveness to her classwork. Soon, though, something outside again caught her attention. Though versions of the story vary, many claim the culprit was a turtle, which she followed outside to play with. One interesting diversion led to another, and soon Catherine had wandered out of sight of the schoolhouse.

When Monsieur Dutarque roused from his reading to find Catherine gone, he panicked, worrying about the dire consequences that would result if the little girl "had fallen into the river, been carried off by a bear, scalped by an Indian, or had bribed the boy Cupid to take her to her aunt's [nearby plantation], where she would probably complain of them, to their great hurt and detriment."[31] He searched every nook and cranny of the house before racing out into the village's streets, trying to find her. After a frightening and frustrating search, Dutarque finally found her safe and sound under the trees of a nearby grove, at which point "a wild and ungovernable rage against the child shook him through and through. As was the measure of his former fears, so was the present measure of his wrath."[32]

Flustered and frightened by Monsieur's angry demeanor, Catherine tried to defend herself, saying that she did not mean to be bad; she had just wanted to spend some time outdoors on such a beautiful day. To which Monsieur Dutarque exclaimed that if it was the outdoors where she wanted to be, then that was where he would leave her. And with that, he snatched the little girl by the arm and took her to nearby Strawberry Chapel, where he tightly tied her to a tombstone to "enjoy" the outdoors for a while.

Here the differing versions of the story provide various reasons for why the schoolmaster did not go back to get Catherine as darkness fell. It's hard to imagine that he actually forgot she was out there, so perhaps it was just meanness on his part that she spent the entire night tied up in the graveyard, undoubtedly recalling the stories she had heard about the Yamasee, who had killed and scalped so many settlers in her grandfather's day, including little girls. She probably also would have feared bears, wolves, and snakes, all of which roamed the woods surrounding Childsbury. Or perhaps she was most frightened of the wandering, long-lost souls of the enslaved who were said to haunt the feared "Robintation Tree" at her stepfather's Comingtee Plantation, where it was said many had been whipped or hanged for their misdeeds. Other versions, including that of Mrs. Rose, relate that a slave, who was sneaking around that night after curfew, passed by the graveyard carrying a gourd or pumpkin with holes cut into it by which a candle dimly illuminated his way, and which to a child would look much like a haunting specter.

Whether some or all of those possibilities were true, the fact is that Catherine was found early the next morning, still tied to the headstone and unresponsive. At first, those who found her thought she was dead, but then someone discerned that she was still breathing, though faintly. She was quickly bundled up and taken to a nearby residence, where she received medical assistance and after a while (some say several days), she regained consciousness.

Even before she was fully lucid, however, Catherine kept repeating that what had happened was not Monsieur Dutarque's fault, that she had misbehaved and all she wanted was to go home, which of course she did. Yet Catherine's family was not feeling nearly as disposed to mercy for the Dutarques as Catherine appeared to be. Though Catherine begged that her teachers' lives be spared, some in the village threatened to hang the schoolmaster. In the end, the matter was settled by ferrying Madame Dutarque across the river and leaving her abandoned there in the Carolina wilderness to face all the threats that Catherine had imagined during her horrific evening in the graveyard. Monsieur Dutarque was run out of town (the best versions of the story claim he was stripped naked, tarred, and feathered tied backward to a mule). Again, the exact details of the Dutarques' fate are undocumented; however, it is true that they never taught or lived in Childsbury again. Documentation suggests that they later worked at another school near Sumter, South Carolina, and that Monsieur went on to work at a boys' school in New Orleans.

Catherine eventually recovered and lived a full life to almost eighty years old. She married Benjamin Simons III of Middleburg Plantation, today the oldest plantation house still standing in either South or North Carolina. Even so, she undoubtedly never forgot the horrific lesson she had learned at Strawberry Chapel about the consequences of misbehaving. Until recently, her portrait remained hanging over the fireplace mantel at Middleburg. The obvious drooping of the left side of her face has led many to believe that the little girl was so frightened that she suffered a stroke that night, resulting in the slight paralysis on her left side.

Today the owners of Strawberry Chapel have had to install protective fencing and security video cameras throughout the churchyard to discourage, catch, and prosecute the vandals who come out to search for the ghost of Little Miss Chicken in the chapel graveyard. Berkeley county sheriff's patrols also keep a close eye on the site. In an effort to discourage vandalism to this remarkable historic landmark, the last remaining vestige of Charles Town's first inland village, it is worth noting that Catherine Chicken Simons (not surprisingly) chose not to be buried in the churchyard founded by her great-grandfather. Instead, her soul rests peacefully with her husband's family elsewhere, in a lovely, open setting with a beautiful view of a Cooper River tributary.

A FINAL NOTE ON STRAWBERRY
CHAPEL'S SPIRITUAL TREASURES

As Union forces bore down on Charleston in February 1865, Keating Simons Ball of Comingtee Plantation, great-grandson of Elias Ball and Lydia Turnsteed Child Chicken Ball (and yes, also related by marriage to, though not directly descended from, Catherine Chicken Simons), along with one of his enslaved workers, gathered up Strawberry Chapel's communion silver to hide it from the invading troops. Their plan was to bury it under the floorboards of Comingtee's rice mill, along the banks of the Cooper River.

Yet after the war was over, the silver was nowhere to be found. Fingers pointed one at another for decades over the loss. Did Keating Simons Ball steal it? Did the now-emancipated slave? Did the Union soldiers find and take it after all? Or did both he and the former slave, as Ball claimed, just forget where they buried it? Whatever he did or didn't know, poor Keating Simons Ball took it to the grave with him in 1891, when he was laid to rest eternally under the oak trees in the Strawberry Chapel churchyard.

From 1927 to 1949, Comingtee Plantation was owned by US senator Joseph S. Frelinghuysen of New Jersey, who used it as a hunting lodge, as so many Northerners of the early twentieth century did with Lowcountry plantation remnants. In late 1946, shortly after World War II, when metal detectors were the cutting-edge technology of the day, Grover and Martha Sullivan, caretakers of Senator Frelinghuysen's Comingtee property, were among the hobbyists who secured one of the coveted detectors from an army surplus sale. With it they began searching for the long-lost communion silver. In a 2017 interview, ninety-seven-year-old Martha Sullivan

The ruins of Comingtee Plantation's rice mill, where Keating Simons Ball is said to have buried the Strawberry silver. *Photo © Leigh Jones Handal*

recalled how seventy years earlier she and her husband would go out in the evenings, scanning the old plantation's terrain with the surplus detector.[33] Sure enough, they eventually got a *ping* near the ruins of what had once been an old plantation barn and began digging.

"The box it had been in had decayed from the wet ground, and we found it piece by piece," Mrs. Sullivan told WCSC reporter Debi Chard.

The recovered chalice and paten are among some of the oldest pieces of Southern silver still existing.[34] Its engraved initials "M.B." on the upper lip of a silver chalice identifies it as the workmanship of Charles Town merchant Miles Brewton. Additional engraving on the set reads "St. John's Parish, in South Carolina, In America." Grahame Long, author of *Stolen Charleston: The Spoils of War*, notes that when the piece was made, probably between 1711 and 1714, many Europeans had not yet heard of South Carolina, and therefore it was necessary to clarify that it came from the New World.

The Sullivans quickly covered the treasure back up until they could safely return it to its rightful owners. For security reasons, the silver is no longer kept on-site at the chapel, but instead is on permanent loan and available for public viewing at the Charleston Museum.

THE CAINHOY MASSACRE

Today State Highway S-8-98, better known locally as Cainhoy Road, is mostly traveled by speeding commuters rushing to their jobs in Mount Pleasant, as well as heavy 18-wheelers serving the industrial complexes tucked away within the forests that line the Wando and Cooper Rivers. Only infrequently does one look carefully enough through the rural highway's bordering tree line to glimpse a small white church set slightly back from the roadside, quietly surrounded by a graveyard dating back to the eighteenth century.

The Church of St. Thomas and St. Denis has a singular history among the ten original parishes established in 1706 that formed the South Carolina colony, for within its geographical borders it served not one but two distinct parishes: one Anglican and one French Huguenot (Calvinist Protestants). Nearly a quarter million Calvinists fled France in the twenty years after 1685, when King Louis XIV revoked the Edict of Nantes, which had granted them freedom of worship in their native country. About five hundred of those refugees came to Charles Town, most settling about twenty-five miles north of the city's wharves, along the fertile grounds nourished by the South Santee River.[35]

The first Church of St. Thomas, built here in 1708 to serve its English-speaking congregation, burned in a forest fire in March 1815 and was replaced by the neoclassical structure one sees there today. Because it was constructed of brick covered in scored stucco and painted white, it became known as "Brick Church" or "White Church" among the wealthy planter families and their enslaved workers who worshipped here. By the time this sanctuary was completed in 1819, members of the area's French-speaking Parish of St. Denis had culturally and linguistically blended and intermarried so thoroughly into English society that the two churches merged within

Founded as one of the original parishes designated by the Church Act of 1706, the Church of St. Thomas and St. Denis was an Anglican parish that absorbed the French Huguenot parish that once shared its geographic boundaries. Today a place of remarkable peace and serenity, the church was the site of one of the deadliest race riots of the 1876 election year. *Library of Congress*

a generation of their founding to form one congregation. The name officially changed in 1784 to the Parish Church of St. Thomas and St. Denis.

Unlike many rural Lowcountry churches, neither St. Thomas and St.
Denis's antebellum sanctuary nor its vestry house, where priests donned
their ministerial robes before services, were burned by Union troops during
the Civil War, though both were battered pretty badly. The nearby rectory,
however, where the Reverend J. Julius Sams lived at the time, did fall victim
to the war's fiery violence.[36]

The decade and a half following the Civil War in South Carolina and
other Southern states was a period of economic, political, and social upheaval
known as Reconstruction, where ideals of racial equality and white supremacy were at war in a redefined country trying to figure out its new norms.
The Civil War may have been over, but the fear, prejudices, hatred, and violence that came with it were still alive and well in Charleston's Lowcountry.
And where there is chaos, there are also opportunities for the self-serving.

Immediately following the end of the Civil War, the state's government was populated to a large degree by so-called Republican carpetbaggers (Northern opportunists who sought to profit from the Reconstruction
government), scalawags (locals who sought to profit by working with their
Northern conquerors against their fellow white Southerners), and both free
and recently emancipated Black people.

Following the period of Reconstruction governmental rule by politicians
who were neither elected from among the Lowcountry's white population
nor represented their interests, the unrest boiled over as white Democrats
struggled to take back control of the state in the elections of 1876. Riots
broke out across South Carolina. One of the most violent, and the only one
that resulted in more white deaths than Black, occurred at the Church of
St. Thomas and St. Denis on October 16, 1876, where once the enslaved
population had worshipped with their plantation masters.

It was the practice of that time for political parties to sponsor "discussion
meetings," similar to what we might call a town hall meeting today.[37] Generally both parties were represented at these meetings. Because tensions were
so high among both Black and white populations in 1876, leaders wisely
decided that no weapons should be brought to the discussion meetings that

year. By "weapons," however, organizers meant long-shooting rifles and shotguns, as virtually everyone routinely carried pistols at that time, particularly as far outside Charleston's urban core as Cainhoy.

Republicans, the vast majority of whom were Black freedmen, called for a party meeting at the parish church. News of the event quickly traveled the twelve miles downriver to Charleston. Although the city of Charleston at that time had a slight majority white population, Charleston County as a whole decidedly had a Black majority of about 3:1. It's estimated that 500 Black Republicans gathered that day at the little brick church, even as 150 white Democrats boarded the steamer *Pocosin* in Charleston and headed upriver to demand equal speaking time at the meeting.[38]

For plenty of good reasons, Black Republicans feared that the white downtown Democrats were coming armed with the intent of causing trouble, though in hindsight, no clear documentation supports that claim. Thus many of the Republicans took precautionary measures, hiding rifles and shotguns in and around the church, in its vestry, in the nearby swamp and woods, and in the new rector's house, which had been rebuilt shortly after its predecessor was burned during the Civil War.

Accounts of what happened next vary in the retelling and according to who tells it. Each side blamed the other for firing the first shot. The prevailing theory is that, on approaching the church, some of the Democrats stumbled across the Republicans' hidden weapons, panicked, and began shooting. Some say the first shot was accidental (others believe it was intentional) and mortally wounded an elderly unarmed Black man standing in the churchyard.

As the greatly outnumbered Democrats began a hasty retreat back to the *Pocosin*, Republicans grabbed their hidden weapons and chased after them. Though the Democrats were not armed (at least to any significant extent), they were, of course, still carrying their pistols and returned fire. One account claims that a white man who tried to escape by climbing up the vestry house's chimney was caught, pulled down, and hacked to pieces. Another story notes that a Colonel Delaney, William E. Simmons, and several other "aged white men" took refuge in the new rector's house, which was riddled with bullet holes. Whatever exactly happened there is undocumented, but blood stains undeniably remained on the attic floor for years afterward. The church's sanctuary quickly became a makeshift hospital, though time, weather, and extensive damage from the Great Earthquake of 1886 have erased any visual evidence of those memories.

Accounts of the number wounded or killed on both sides vary widely— from sixteen to more than fifty. In the end, at least five or six documented white Democrats lay dead in the churchyard and surrounding marsh, as did the elderly Black man who was said to have been the first person shot. Even with that lowest count, the Cainhoy Massacre at the Church of St. Thomas and St. Denis became the only incident during the race riots of 1876 that resulted in more white deaths than Black. When the news reached Columbia, South Carolina governor Daniel Henry Chamberlain ordered Federal troops to Charleston to prevent further violence until the elections were concluded.

Rarely used after the Civil War and the fall of the Lowcountry's plantation society, the Church of St. Thomas and St. Denis has been mostly forgotten and quietly deteriorating over the years. Some recalled a time when goats made their home in the church; during Prohibition moonshiners hid their whiskey stashes here. In 1937 New York industrial mogul Henry F. Guggenheim, who then owned much of the old Cainhoy peninsula and used it as a seasonal vacation home and hunting preserve, restored the church, which greatly contributed to its preservation for a while. Today, a local vestry of committed volunteers still keep its maintenance up and its history alive as best they can. The church and its graveyard were listed on the National Register of Historic Places in 1977.

THE HOPES AND HORRORS OF HAMPTON PARK

oday's Hampton Park is a sixty-acre site operated by the City of Charleston as a passive municipal garden, located adjacent to The Citadel in the northwest corner of the peninsular city. On any given day, cyclists, joggers, and dog walkers enjoy taking laps around the roughly one-mile paved drive that encircles the garden's vignettes.

Yet the history behind this idyllic site is filled not only with breathtakingly beautiful spring blooms, outdoor weddings, and family picnics but also with war, inhumanity, death, and destruction—for these grounds have at various times served as a colonial pleasure garden, a farm, a siege camp, a dueling site, the epicenter of Charleston's antebellum social life, a barbaric prisoner of war camp, an Ivory City of hope and economic promise, and a failed, inhumane zoo.

The site encompasses stories from all periods of Charleston's history and is a case study of historical contrasts. It is named for Wade Hampton, a Confederate general who served as the state's governor from 1877 to 1879 and its US senator from 1879 to 1891, and whose historical legacy today is associated—rightly or wrongly—with the Red Shirts, a paramilitary political party that used violence and intimidation to suppress the post-Reconstruction Black Republican vote. Within the park stands the city's memorial statue honoring Denmark Vesey, an enslaved carpenter who bought his freedom with lottery winnings and whose historical legacy today is associated—rightly or wrongly—with an 1822 plot to kill every white man, woman, and child to be found on Charleston's streets. Though controversy surrounds the diverse interpretations and veracity of the documentation, details, and historical retellings of these two men's stories, most people can agree that honoring them at the same site is, at the least, an interesting contrast.[1]

Controversial ironies aside, the park's earliest recorded history, based on archeological research, has found no evidence that Native Americans ever established any long-term settlements here. According to Kevin R. Eberle, author of *A History of Charleston's Hampton Park*, that's not too surprising given that within the twenty-nine tribes who inhabited South Carolina in the late seventeenth century, probably fewer than two thousand Natives, mostly associated with the Muskogean and Siouan nations, lived along the state's coastline, making it easy to space out settlements and hunting grounds with only rare disputes or confrontations.[2]

The Lowcountry's Natives were nomadic and moved around the area in accord with the seasons and availability of their food sources. Summer generally found them along the coast's edge, fishing and harvesting oysters and clams. The women would plant a few rudimentary crops such as corn and sweet potatoes, but never developed any sophisticated cultivation processes. If the seeds grew where they fell, they grew; if not, they didn't. When the weather became cooler in the fall, one or more families within a tribe would move inland together to hunt deer and other game before returning to the general area of their coastal homes in the spring.[3]

At the urging of the Cassique, chief of the Kiawah confederacy of tribes, Charles Town's earliest English settlers established their first village in 1670 near the Native American settlement at Albemarle Point, located along the west bank of the Ashley River across from the neighborhood we now associate with Hampton Park. Today that site has become Charles Towne Landing State Park, where archaeologists have found evidence of postholes and pottery remnants, suggesting that the location has been intermittently inhabited since perhaps 500 BC.

A bluff along the east side of the Ashley River there features the highest point of land in peninsular Charleston, rising about fifteen feet above sea level, a virtual mountain for low-lying Charleston. Early maps referred to this bluff as "Indian Hill," located adjacent to where The Citadel's student cafeteria, Coward Hall, is today.

For many years, local lore held that Indian Hill was a haunted Native American burial ground. That myth was debunked, however, in 1962 by archaeologist Stanley A. South. While South found no grave remains on Indian Hill, he did find evidence of early colonial settlement, including the foundation of two brick buildings, a wine bottle, pipes, pottery, a nail, and a buckle—all probably dating between 1689 and 1720.

Eberle has traced the earliest documented European ownership of Hampton Park to a land grant of 423 acres given by King Charles II to Joseph Dalton, who arrived aboard the *Carolina*, the first ship to land here in April 1670. About thirty years later, and certainly by the time Edward Crisp created his map of the area in 1711, about 190 acres of Dalton's land, including Hampton Park, had been acquired by Daniel Cartwright. He in turn sold the tract to John Braithwaite on May 8, 1738.[4]

By 1769, John Gibbes owned the area bounded today by Congress Street on the south and including Hampton Park, the Hampton Park Terrace neighborhood, The Citadel, Lowndes Grove, and parts of the Wagener Terrace neighborhood. His plantation became known as Orange Grove, sometimes shortened to just The Grove. Based on a 1780s map, Gibbes's main house was located in front of where The Citadel's Summerall Chapel stands today and was surrounded by extensive gardens and support buildings.[5]

Fifty years later, as he was penning reminiscences of his years as a soldier under the command of Maj. Gen. Henry "Light Horse Harry" Lee III and aide-de-camp to Gen. Nathanael Greene, Alexander Garden described Gibbes's garden in some detail. Garden was not only the grandson of the botanist for whom the gardenia was named, but also the husband of John Gibbes's niece. The Grove, he said, had been "improved not only with taste in the disposition of the grounds, but by the introduction of numberless exotics of the highest beauty. . . . [John Gibbes] had, in addition, a green-house and pinery, in the best condition."[6] (*Pinery* refers to a hothouse built specifically for growing pineapples.) Garden's description of Grove Plantation is, however, as Eberle notes, perhaps of more value to botanical historians than the

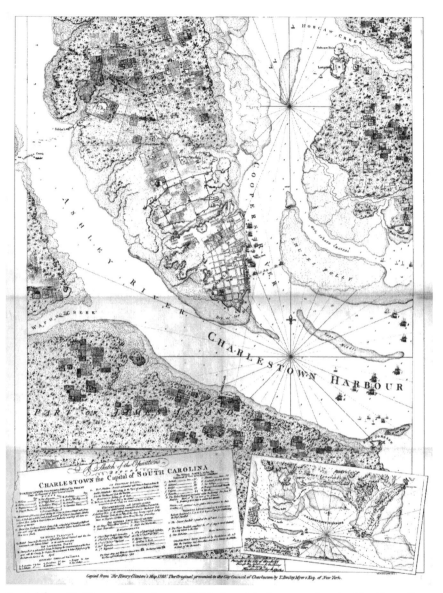

Copied from Sir Henry Clinton's map, 1780; the original presented to the City Council of Charleston by T. Bailey Myers, Esq., of New York. This image shows the elaborately designed gardens and buildings of John Gibbes's Grove Plantation, the staging site for the British Siege of Charleston, as well as Gibbes Landing, where Clinton's army came ashore. *WikiMedia Commons*

remainder of his rather romantic and somewhat dramatized account of the American Revolution is to historical scholars.[7]

JOHN GIBBES' CURSE AND THE SIEGE OF CHARLES TOWN

Much to Gen. Sir Henry Clinton's frustration, the British were never able to take Charles Town by sea. Thus, in February 1780, Clinton landed his troops about thirty miles south of the city, advancing on foot first to James Island and then northwest along the Ashley River to Drayton Hall, strategically situated just above and across the river from John Gibbes's Orange Grove plantation. Crossing the Ashley in March of that year, Clinton set up camp near what today is Grove Street (hence its name) and began bringing his troops over at Gibbes's river landing. In his journal, a Hessian sharpshooter named Capt. Johann Ewald relates landing at The Grove, where he "did picket duty in one of the most beautiful pleasure gardens of the world."[8]

The next day Captain Ewald wrote, "The county around Gibbes' house has been made a park and depot for the siege, and the greenhouse is a laboratory." His company was ordered to advance "through the wood in front of

Johann von Ewald, c. 1835, print by C. A. Jensen, made from a drawing by H. J. Aldenrath. Shown here in his later years attired in his general's uniform, then-captain Johann Ewald chronicled the destruction of The Grove plantation during the Siege of Charleston in his soldier's journal. *WikiMedia Commons*

Gibbes' house and through the swamp on the left bank of the Ashley River." Gibbes's property suffered significant damage as a result, Ewald wrote: "Major Moncrieff of the Engineers had all the wooden houses in the neighborhood torn down today. From the boards and beams of these he had his men make mantelets [e.g., bullet blockers] to be used in building the inner side of the batteries and redoubts and also the cheeks of the embrasures."

While all of this mayhem was going on, John Gibbes was out of town visiting his brother, Robert. When a British soldier identified only as Major Sheridan arrived at Robert Gibbes's home, Gibbes asked whether the city had fallen yet. According to Garden's memoirs, Major Sheridan, not aware that he was speaking in front of The Grove's owner, responded, "I fear not, but we have made glorious havoc of the property in the vicinity. . . . I yesterday witnessed the destruction of an elegant establishment belonging to a Rebel, who luckily for himself was absent. You would have been delighted to see how quickly the pine apples [sic] were shared among our men, and how rapidly his trees and ornamental shrubs were leveled with the dust."[9]

According to Garden's memoir, John Gibbes immediately recognized that Sheridan was talking about his plantation and responded, "I hope that the Almighty will cause the arm of the scoundrel who struck the first blow to wither to his shoulder." After which, Garden claims, John Gibbes retired to his bed and died.

ANTEBELLUM GRANDEUR: OF HORSES AND BALLS AND MEETING THE RIGHT SORT OF PEOPLE

John Gibbes had no children, and so upon his death, his brother, Robert, divided Grove Plantation into twenty-seven lots, ranging in size from three to twelve acres each, and listed them for sale. Along the northern edge of the property, a large tract (lots 18, 19, and 20) was sold to George Abbot Hall, who developed it into Lowndes Grove Plantation, the same name by which we know it today. According to Hall's 1791 inventory,[10] the house was built around 1786, four years after the British left Charleston, having lost the American War for Independence, yet pretty much destroying everything that John Gibbes had created in his garden paradise.

In August of that same year, 1791, the South Carolina Jockey Club purchased the tract we now know as Hampton Park to build a new horse racing track. Like their namesake King Charles II, eighteenth- and nineteenth-century Charlestonians had few greater passions than horse racing. Racing played an important role in Charleston's social life, and the South Carolina Jockey Club, America's first, was organized in 1758. Among its elite membership were Gen. Charles Cotesworth Pinckney, delegate to the Constitutional Convention of 1787 and principal author of "The Pinckney Draft" of the US Constitution; Brig. Gen. William Washington, hero of the Battle of Cowpens; and Gen. William Moultrie, South Carolina governor and Revolutionary War hero of the Battle of Sullivan's Island, the British Navy's first major naval defeat of the Revolution.

They named the new course for William Washington's cousin George, who had visited the city and viewed the site of the new racetrack earlier that year. From its first race on February 15, 1792, until its interruption by the Civil War, the course's one-mile loop featured the finest horse racing in the South for the next seven decades.

The Jockey Club's annual Race Week, held each February, marked the pinnacle of Charleston's social season throughout the antebellum period. Here the great Lowcountry planters gathered to show their horses, make bets, attend balls, close business deals, drink fine Madeira wine, and introduce their daughters to the right sort of people in the reserved seating sections. Race Week was, as Jockey Club historian John Beaufain Irving described it in 1857, the "carnival of the state."[11]

Inns, restaurants, and taverns sprung up all around the course. Affluent members of the Jockey Club hosted elaborate dinners and a Friday night ball each year. Much like during today's annual Spoleto Festival, the South of Broad crowd would host grand balls and events for their out-of-town guests with advantageous social connections and heirs of marriageable age.

In the 1830s the track was enclosed by a tall fence, ensuring that only those who paid admission could view the races. Always a socially conscious group, however, the Jockey Club made it a policy that "respectable strangers from abroad or from other states are never allowed to pay admission . . . they are considered guests."[12] In the late 1840s, the Jockey Club purchased a twenty-three-acre farm adjoining the course to provide stabling and pastures for out-of-town guests.

Similar to the horse races held in Charleston and Camden today, actually watching the horses was but one small part of what made Race Week so special. While ladies generally remained in their designated grandstand, designed by renowned architect Charles Reichart in 1836, the gentlemen wandered the grounds freely, mixing raucously with gamblers, the enslaved, traveling salesmen, and others who were excluded from the more refined areas of the course. The infield and areas surrounding the track provided a range of entertainment and sales opportunities, including public auctions of real estate, horses, and slaves. Contemporary news accounts share stories of popular amusements such as military demonstrations; the "Learned Pig," whose intellectual prowess was advertised in both 1799 and 1804;[13] or the sale of imported Thoroughbreds.

Though owners occasionally rode their own horses in the races, most of the jockeys were enslaved. Breeders relied on the abilities of their slaves to breed, train, and ride their horses to victory. Col. William Alston, a member of the Jockey Club, had a cup commissioned sometime after 1810, the date inscribed on it along with his initials and part of the Alston family crest. The cup, now displayed at the Nathaniel Russell House, a house museum open to the public at 51 Meeting Street, has been in the Alston family for eight generations. According to family lore, it was commissioned by Alston after his mare Betsy Baker was victorious over a horse named Rosetta that year.

Because the Washington Race Course was an open space and remotely located (at least as the city's boundaries existed in the nineteenth century), it provided a good setting for duels when it was not being used for races. Numerous duels—some fatal, most not—were recorded in local news accounts. When the course wasn't being used for such exciting activities as racing or dueling, neighborhood farmers would lease the grounds to graze their livestock.

THE SHOT HEARD 'ROUND THE WORLD,
WHICH CHANGED EVERYTHING

But the fun and games ended with the first shot of the Civil War, fired just a few weeks after John Cantey's mare Albine won the 1861 heat. The races took a hiatus, and the Washington Race Course was repurposed to house Union prisoners of war. Officers were quartered in the filthy, bug-infested former Ladies Club, ironically once the site of Charleston's most gracious social fetes. Conditions in the mostly open-air camp were horrendous; 257 Union soldiers' deaths were recorded, and surely there were many others. Prisoners died so quickly and in such great numbers that their Confederate guards could not keep up with the needed burials. Many corpses were unceremoniously rolled into large ditches and covered over in mass unmarked graves.

Shortly after the city fell to Union forces in February 1865, the men of several Black church congregations returned to the racetrack where, over the course of several weeks, they exhumed the mass burial ditches and, this time with respect and honor, reburied in individual graves the Union soldiers who had died fighting for their freedom. Bodies that still had some sort of identification on them were given headstones. Those that did not at least were marked with crosses. After they were finished, the freedmen erected a fence around the site with a gate that read "Martyrs of the Race Course."

Union officers were held captive in the Ladies Club of the Washington Race Course. Ironically, the site of some of Charleston's finest social fetes was now the site of suffering and death. *Library of Congress*

145

Newly emancipated freedmen respectfully reinterred the bodies of Union soldiers who had died fighting for their freedom at the Washington Race Course prison camp, April 1865. Many credit this event as being among the first, if not the first, Memorial Day celebrations. *Library of Congress*

Upon completing the mammoth task, on May 1, 1865, ten thousand emancipated African Americans marched in a parade from downtown to the Washington Race Course, according to the *Charleston Daily Courier*:

The exercises on the ground commenced with reading a Psalm, singing a hymn, followed by a prayer. The procession was formed shortly after nine o'clock, and made a beautiful appearance, nearly every one present bearing a handsome boquet [sic] of flowers. The colored children, about twenty-eight hundred in number, marched first over the burial ground, strewing the graves with their flowers as they passed. . . . These were followed by the citizens generally, nearly all with boquets, which were also laid upon the graves. While standing around the graves the school children sung, "The Star Spangled Banner," "America" and "Rally Round the Flag," and while marching, "John Brown's Body, &c." The graves at the close of the procession had all the appearance of a mass of roses.[14]

Civil War historian David Bright notes: "The symbolic power of the low-country planter aristocracy's horse track (where they had displayed their wealth, leisure, and influence) was not lost on the freedpeople."[15] He quotes a *New York Tribune* correspondent who witnessed the event, describing it as "a procession of friends and mourners as South Carolina and the United States never saw before."

Emancipated women spread out their blankets and served a massive communal picnic for the participants. At the time, locals referred to the day's events as Decoration Day—and though a handful of communities across America contend that their citizens were responsible for organizing the first Memorial Day, many scholars credit this as that holiday's true first celebration.

In 1871 the bodies of the Union soldiers were again exhumed and reburied for the third time with honors at military cemeteries in Florence and Beaufort, both in South Carolina. The racetrack resumed its use as a quiet pasture for grazing livestock.

THE SECOND HEAT

The last four decades of the nineteenth century were singularly miserable for Charlestonians. The Great Fire of 1861 actually did more damage to the city's downtown than even four years of Union bombardment, which wasn't pretty either. The crushed city was then subject to Federal occupation and Reconstruction government through 1877.

In 1875, however, the South Carolina Jockey Club, determined to pull through the calamities that had befallen their city, reorganized. Though money was tight, the club still had two major assets. The first was the racetrack itself and the land around it. The second was a cache of valuable Madeira wine that had somehow miraculously escaped discovery and plunder by Union troops. Proceeds from the sale of the Madeira, along with the recruitment of one hundred members, revived the Washington races.

As the 1880s loomed on the horizon, other Charlestonians likewise began taking their first steps toward pulling themselves together again. Having gathered up the strewn and damaged bricks of the Circular Congregational Church, destroyed by both the 1861 fire and Union cannon shells, members began rebuilding the edifice on the remains of its historic foundation. Well before completing the work, however, those bricks too came crashing down a second time as the largest earthquake to ever strike the East Coast (estimated to have been between a 7.2 and 7.4 on today's Richter scale) rumbled underneath the city, its epicenter estimated to be only about ten miles up the Ashley River, at approximately the site where Sir Henry Clinton had crossed the river to land his troops at John Gibbes's Grove Plantation in 1780. Charlestonians were still surveying the damage when, over the next fourteen years, seven hurricanes blew through the city: one in 1885, two in 1893, another in both 1894 and 1896, and finally two more in 1898.

If the last half of the nineteenth century had been devastating to Charlestonians in general, so it was to the South Carolina Jockey Club. Breeding racehorses is a rich man's sport, and few wealthy men were left in Charleston after the Civil War. Grand balls and high style were no longer the order of the day. Race Week had forever lost its cachet, and attendance after the war never came close to its antebellum heyday. Two years after its last race in 1882, the Jockey Club leased the racecourse, its surrounding pastures, and stables to farmer J. H. West to graze his animals. In 1899, with only about two dozen members remaining, America's first racing club disbanded, donating their few remaining assets, including the Washington Race Course, to the Charleston Library Society.

Charlestonians desperately needed a sense of renewed hope and optimism for the future, and that hope came in the form of the South Carolina Inter-State and West Indian Exposition of 1901–1902.

THE IVORY CITY

Even as the Jockey Club disbanded, a handful of mostly young, enterprising businessmen sought a way to stimulate Charleston's flagging fortunes, particularly in industry and trade. In colonial times, Charles Town had stood on the western terminus of the great Atlantic coastal highway. Ships dependent on wind power followed the natural trade winds from Europe to the West Indies, where they picked up the Gulf Stream currents that conveniently deposited them into Charleston Harbor. With the advent of the steam engine in the 1820s, however, ships no longer had to rely on these natural navigational resources and Charleston's port began to lose business. Exposition organizers hoped to "rebrand," as we might call it today, Charleston as America's leading port of foreign trade, as it had been in the days of the pirates.

A number of grand fairs in such places as London, Atlanta, and New Orleans had successfully extolled the virtues of their local goods, talents, and commercial resources to the world, and the Charleston group looked to them for ideas and inspiration. Chief among the leaders of the effort was Capt. Frederick C. Wagener, a German immigrant, local businessman, and editor of the *Charleston News and Courier.*

At Wagener's urging, in 1900, a year after the Jockey Club's donation, the Charleston Library Society leased the Washington Race Course to the organizers of the South Carolina Inter-State and West Indian Exposition. Captain Wagener, at that time the owner of the adjacent Lowndes Grove Plantation, added his property to the mix to create about 250 acres for the fair. Daily news coverage of the exposition exceeded mere hyperbole and served as a powerful marketing tool for the undertaking. After a year of fundraising and planning, the resources were in place to begin creating Charleston's twentieth-century world debut event.

Organizers hired Bradford Lee Gilbert, a New York–based architect who had been involved with the Atlanta exposition several years earlier, to design and oversee construction of the exposition's elaborate "palaces." Gilbert painted all the buildings, most of which he designed in the exotic Spanish Renaissance style, in a creamy off-white color with distinctive contrasting detailing, leading to the expo's nickname, the "Ivory City." After more than a year of massive construction, the South Carolina Inter-State and West Indian Exposition opened amid great fanfare on December 2, 1901, with an estimated twenty-two thousand people in attendance. Some reports note that even Samuel Clemens, better known as author Mark Twain, attended.

The most prominent among the exhibit halls was the Cotton Palace, at 320 feet long with a grand 75-foot-tall dome and 50,000 square feet of exhibit space. Other key buildings included the Hall of Fisheries, Hall of Machinery, Hall of Mines and Forestry, Hall for Women, Hall for Negroes, Hall of Administration, and the Auditorium. Twenty states were represented, as well as the cities of Cincinnati and Philadelphia, the latter proudly displaying the Liberty Bell.

Everywhere the grounds were adorned with statuary. The exposition's popular midway included a carnival, rides, Eskimo Village, Turkish Parlor, animal acts, exotic dancers, and a House of Horrors. To top it all off, visitors could enjoy the show both day and night, as modern electric lighting was used throughout the venues. Yet most historians agree that perhaps the Ivory City's grandest feature was its sunken gardens, with its fountains, bridges, and pools that ran throughout the main venue linking the four principal palaces.

Even so, a plethora of problems plagued the exposition from its beginning. Many exhibits from abroad that had been envisioned never materialized, and only twenty states and two other American cities were represented. Many exhibits were installed late and hastily, some even opening after the exposition had begun.

A panoramic view of three of the four principal palaces of the South Carolina Inter-State and West Indian Exposition's Ivory City. Taken from the perspective of the central village's Auditorium, from left to right are the South Carolina Building, the Cotton Palace, and the Palace of Commerce. The Bandstand is featured in the center of the park's elaborate sunken gardens. *Library of Congress*

The Cotton Palace was the most impressive of the exposition's buildings, with more than fifty thousand square feet of exhibition space. *Library of Congress*

A view of the sunken gardens, looking north toward the Auditorium. *Library of Congress*

The exposition's midway featured carnival rides, exotic animal exhibits, an Eskimo Village, a Turkish Parlor, exotic dancers, and a House of Horrors. *Library of Congress*

Exposition organizers created a new racecourse slightly north of the original Washington Race Course. *Library of Congress*

And finally, at the risk of understatement, it was a bad year for the weather, with a cold, dreary, and rainy spring for Charleston's normally sub-tropical climate. Almost unbelievably, the December 2, 1901, opening day of the exposition was marred by the arrival of a late-season tropical storm, blowing in after what traditionally is considered the last day of the annual Atlantic hurricane season. Perhaps even more unbelievably, the last nail in the exposition's coffin came when another storm blew through the Low-country on May 31, one day before at the traditional June 1 start of the tropical storm season. With this final setback, the exposition closed, barely halfway through its expected yearlong run.

Despite the *News and Courier*'s daily headlines touting its grandeur, the exposition was a huge financial failure. While organizers considered daily attendance to be good with about 674,086 recorded paying visitors, includ-ing a gala visit from President Theodore Roosevelt, revenues fell far short of expectations. Construction of the Ivory City had cost $1.25 million; gate receipts were a humble $313,000. Perhaps most disappointing, the grand effort lured only two businesses to Charleston: the American Cigar Com-pany and a mattress manufacturer.

Today the South Carolina Inter-State and West Indian Exposition has been largely forgotten among the international list of great world fairs. Charleston's magnificent Ivory City was quickly torn down and auctioned off for whatever price its raw materials could bring in an effort to offset some of the debt.

Later that year, the City of Charleston purchased the Washington Race Course from the Charleston Library Society for $32,500 to redevelop as a municipal park. They named it Hampton Park, for the state's governor who sought to suppress Black Republican voting.

Little remains today of the Ivory City, though a few subtle reminders can be found for those who know their history well enough to recognize them. A section of the palaces' sunken gardens was retained and today serves as a duck pond, though often the avian excrement prevents visitors from getting too close lest they dispel the idyllic image one can still enjoy from afar. A rather small, humble building that had served as the Wayside Inn, an exhibit featuring early American colonial life, was left standing and has been repurposed as storage space for the city's parks and horticultural staff.

The gates that once proclaimed and honored the "Martyrs of the Race-course" became surplus property. In 1903 August Belmont Jr., a New York racehorse owner and part-time South Carolina resident, asked to buy the four remaining gate posts. Instead, the City of Charleston simply offered them to him as a gift. The posts were boxed and shipped to Long Island, where they were repaired and installed at the new Belmont Park. On the track's opening day, May 4, 1906, almost forty years to the day after the freedmen's Decoration Day celebration, nearly forty thousand people streamed through the South Carolina Jockey Club's gates at their new New York home, without anyone even knowing the significance of their history. They remain visible there today for those traveling in from the New Jersey Turnpike.

THE ZOO

During the mid-twentieth century, the park featured a small zoo. According to Eberle's research, the first documented reference to there being animals at the park was in 1909, when swans appeared in the sunken garden. Three years later, a few alligators joined them. Soon the zoo's annual inventory grew to include "two pairs of hoot owls, a pair of prairie dogs, pheasants and a black swan."[16] By 1929, more exotic as well as indigenous animals had joined the menagerie, including fourteen monkeys, two gray foxes, one red fox, one coyote, three parrots, two honey bears, five deer, three goats, six sheep, two peacocks, four owls, two pheasants, two fox squirrels, three raccoons, and twenty-five rabbits.[17] Perhaps most famous, however, thanks in part to the novels of author and former Citadel cadet Pat Conroy, was the lion, who could be heard roaring his lonely outrage throughout nearby neighborhoods in the quiet evenings.

In a fashion reminiscent of the 1865 Decoration Day, families would come to the park with picnics and blankets, maybe take in a Citadel dress parade if it was a Friday. Admission to the zoo was free, and the city maintained the property with big, open-air spaces. The zoo peaked in the 1940s and 1950s, until the desegregation of, and ensuing white flight from, the city's upper peninsula area. The less financial support the zoo made through its concession stands, the shabbier it got. Ultimately, the zoo failed to meet the national standards established by the Animal Welfare Act of 1971. Rather than renovate to improve its facilities, the city decided to close the zoo. Though little documentation exists, the animals were either given away or set loose.

TODAY

Today the oval track of the Washington Race Course exists as Mary Murray Boulevard, paved and renamed for his beloved wife in 1924 by philanthropist and former ward of the Charleston Orphan House, Andrew Buist Murray, to better accommodate the newfangled automobiles. New gate posts have replaced the ones that have now stood at the Belmont Race Course for more than 115 years. Ducks still swim in the sunken pools under the moss-draped live oaks that have grown huge, relatively undisturbed over the past century. Especially in spring, there are few places prettier or better for a picnic than the park that stands on the site of John Gibbes's old pleasure garden. Hopefully his spirit again rests well.

THE TAIL OF WASHINGTON'S HORSE

Since its first session in 1818 at Charleston City Hall, located at the historic intersection of Broad and Meeting Streets, City Council has met in the same black walnut desks in what is now the second-oldest municipal council chamber in America to have been in continuous use. The chamber is beautiful, with antebellum chandeliers, original 1896 Thomas Edison lightbulbs that softly lit the room until 1983, an ornate cast-iron railing surrounding an upper-level visitors' gallery, and a hand-painted tin ceiling. Its warm, wood-paneled walls are resplendent with historical artwork, perhaps the most renowned of which is a life-size portrait of President George Washington painted in 1792 by his aide-de-camp and friend Col. John Trumbull (1756–1843).

Yet it takes the observant viewer only a few moments of study to realize that the painting—to put it mildly although candidly—offers admirers a distinctly unique perspective: Washington's horse, whose hind end is prominently displayed with its tail raised in anticipation, appears about to defecate on the city itself, its skyline positioned in the distance right beneath the equine's back legs.

Was the implication intentional? An insult to the city? An inside joke? An oversight? Just an artist's interpretation with no particular meaning? Tour guides and City Hall docents have for decades claimed that Trumbull meant the image as a snub to Charleston's city fathers, who rejected his first painting and sent it back.[1] Yet recent research by Dr. Nicholas Butler, historian with the Charleston County Public Library and the creator of the CCPL

General George Washington at Trenton by artist John Trumbull (1756–1843), c. 1792; oil on canvas. Gift of the Society of the Cincinnati in the State of Connecticut; currently at Yale University. *WikiMedia Commons*

Charleston Time Machine podcasts, has produced new details that indicate the story might not be so open-and-shut as that.

Trumbull was a widely recognized and respected painter around the time of the American Revolution, after which he painted many of its distinguished heroes, including several portraits of Washington. Trumbull had been in Charleston shortly before the president's historic visit in May 1791, painting commissions for local luminaries, including members of the Pinckney, Middleton, Rutledge, Heyward, and Laurens families.[2]

Charlestonians were wildly excited about the president's visit and went out of their way to demonstrate it. They crowded the city's bunting-lined streets, loudly cheered his arrival at the wharf at the end of Vendue Lane, and staged nightly balls in his honor. They invited him to lay the cornerstone for the city's new orphanage (the first public institution of its kind in America). The prestigious South Carolina Jockey Club named their new horse racing track, the Washington Race Course, after him. And shortly after the president's departure, South Carolina congressman William Loughton Smith, on behalf of the Charleston City Council, commissioned John Trumbull for a portrait to commemorate the visit.[3]

Happily accepting the commission, Trumbull thoughtfully decided to depict Washington as he remembered seeing him in 1777, the evening before the Second Battle of Trenton, New Jersey, a turning point of the Revolution.[4] It portrays Washington in full military uniform, a telescope in one hand, a sword at the ready in the other. Behind him his well-recognized gray horse, Blueskin, rears up in anxious anticipation of the coming battle, and in the distance, one can just make out the American flag flying amid the soldiers' encampment.

In his 1841 memoir, Trumbull described the painting as "the best certainly of those which I painted, and the best, in my estimation, which exists, in his heroic military character. The City of Charleston, S.C., instructed William R. [sic] Smith, one of the representatives of South Carolina, to employ me to paint for them a portrait of the great man, and I undertook it con amore, meaning to give his military character, in the most sublime moment of its exertion—the evening previous to the battle of Princeton; . . . I told the president my object; he entered into it warmly, and, as the work advanced, we talked of the scene, its dangers, its almost desperation. He looked the scene again, and I happily transferred to the canvas, the lofty expression of his animated countenance, the high resolve to conquer or to perish. The result was in my own opinion eminently successful, and the general was satisfied."[5]

But Congressman Smith was not satisfied and rejected the painting. Trumbull's memoir continues: "But it did not meet the views of Mr. Smith. He admired it, he was personally pleased, but he thought the city would be better satisfied with a more matter-of-fact likeness, such as they had recently seen him—calm, tranquil, peaceful." Smith asked Trumbull to do a new painting, this time with Charleston as the setting. Trumbull agreed, and the president graciously agreed to sit a second time. Trumbull donated the original portrait to the Society of Cincinnati, who in turn eventually donated it to Yale University, where it hangs today.

The second painting, titled *Washington at the City of Charleston*, depicts the president standing at Haddrell's Point, across Charleston Harbor in

Washington at the City of Charleston, 1792, a reworking of *General George Washington at Trenton* by John Trumbull (1756–1842), as seen today in Charleston City Hall. *WikiMedia Commons*

neighboring Mount Pleasant, with a magnificent view of the city's eastern waterfront. The inclusion of palmetto palms and local plants clearly denotes the location. In very similar attire to the first painting (except that the buttons on the jacket are reversed) Washington casually holds a walking stick in his right hand and his hat in his left, which rests on his sheathed sword by his side. Indeed, this was a more "calm, tranquil and peaceful" image of General Washington and clearly set in Charleston, as Congressman Smith had requested.

Here the popular legend asserts that Trumbull was secretly angry about the rejection of his first portrait and therefore, after City Council had approved and paid for the second portrait, Trumbull said he would deliver it as soon as he finished a few small details. At that point, the artist went back and maliciously sketched in the horse assuming the posture previously described.[6]

Butler notes, however, that no documentation exists to support this popular version of the story. Unfortunately, nearly all of the city's governmental records, which might have included a bill of sale or City Council minutes regarding the portrait, were destroyed in the fires, destruction, looting, and chaos that ensued when the city fell to Union troops in 1865. Any minutes from 1792 were undoubtedly destroyed long ago, along with any documentation of exactly when and with what enthusiasm or comment the City Council accepted the portrait.

Butler also points out a couple of other pertinent details: First, it was Congressman Smith, not the City Council, who rejected the first portrait. Indeed there's no indication it was ever even seen by the City Council, thus Trumbull would have no cause to be miffed with the city fathers. Was Trumbull angry with Smith for rejecting his first painting? Nothing in the historical record—neither his letters to Smith, the president, or others—indicates any hard feelings over the situation. Smith and Trumbull were, and apparently remained, friends both before and after the portrait's commission.[7] Indeed, Smith commissioned the artist to paint his own likeness shortly afterward, which Trumbull did with no hint of malice. They had been friends before the city's Washington commission, and by all accounts remained so afterward.

South Carolina congressman William L Smith by John Trumbull,
American (1756–1843); oil on wood, painted c. 1792. *Yale
University Art Gallery*

Today it's probably safe to assume we will never know if the horse's
threatening rear end was added by a miffed artist after the portrait's acceptance or if the city fathers just missed seeing an implication that seems quite
evident to many. Historian and author T. H. Breen shares Butler's caution
that no actual documentation exists to confirm that the City Council was
displeased with the second portrait or that Trumbull ever expressed any
enmity about having his first effort rejected.[8] Documentation aside, however, in the final analysis Breen notes: "But just look at it."

CHARLESTON'S PUBLIC SQUARE: HELL, WICKED PLACES, AND SOME REALLY GREAT JAZZ

No other spot within Charleston's Old and Historic District has crueler or more inhumane stories to tell than a small, unassuming block located almost in the center of the peninsular city, bounded today by Magazine, Logan, Queen, and Franklin Streets. Many have claimed to sense the cold aura of death, despair, and hopelessness emanating from this relatively unattractive parcel of land tucked amid downtown's beautiful gardens and streetscapes, even those who are unfamiliar with its history. Something of that legacy carries over even to today, as the historic buildings that remain on this site abut an urban public housing project built in 1939.

Untold thousands have suffered and died within this four-acre parcel. Many of their bones lie here subterraneously as well, unceremoniously interred in unmarked graves on land designated for public use by Lord Proprietor Anthony Ashley Cooper and his secretary, John Locke, in their 1680 "Grande Modell of Charles Town." Here, not too far outside the early colony's fortified walls, Cooper and Locke set aside public land that would one day house a jail, a poorhouse for debtors and a workhouse for the enslaved, a hospital, a lunatic asylum, a paupers' graveyard, and a powder magazine for the storage of gunpowder and munitions.

Shortly after the colonists moved from their original settlement at Albemarle Point to today's peninsular city in 1680, the lot began being used as a public cemetery.[1] Yet as the colonists began building new churches, first St. Philip's Anglican in 1680 and the Dissenters' Meeting House the year thereafter, families increasingly buried their dead in the hallowed grounds of their respective churchyards. In addition, as plantations developed, many of Charles Town's planters' aristocracy, as well as their enslaved workers, were buried in family cemeteries on their private estates.

As more colonists began to be buried elsewhere, the need for the public cemetery decreased and it became used primarily for the interment of "strangers": mariners and visitors from out of town or basically anyone who did not have an affiliation with local churches. As the old cemetery came to be used less, it also became less well maintained. In November 1743, a grand jury complained to the provincial government "that ye Old Church Yard, or burying place in Charles Town is very much neglected and that all manner of filth, & nastyness is thrown into the graves and vaults of the deceased, whereby the surviving relations of the deceased are very much troubled and grieved."[2]

As use of the public cemetery decreased, Charles Town's Provincial Assembly began to construct additional public facilities on the block, undoubtedly right over the graves of many long buried and forgotten there. The first of these was a new powder magazine, completed in 1737 on its northwest corner. Though this magazine remained there for only a couple of years, its presence is recalled in the name of the block's northern boundary, Magazine Street.

A facility to house the poor and homeless was completed a year later on the plat's northeastern corner. Before the American Revolution, the Church of England was South Carolina's officially sanctioned state church, and as such it was largely responsible for the care and welfare of orphans, the poor, and those deemed insane or physically disabled. Church members would either take in these wretched souls themselves or hire someone to provide them with the basics of shelter, food, water, and clothing. Before 1738, however, a grand jury in Charles Town determined that "private dwellings rented for the sick and poor were inadequate, dilapidated, and costly," leading to the establishment of a building to house the poor and "to punish idle and disorderly people," providing "a controlled environment to regulate the morals of the uninhibited."[3] The first building constructed for this purpose was completed in 1738; however, it was replaced within thirty years because of "putrid smells, filthy, crowded rooms and indiscriminate mixing of poor widows, prostitutes, and thieves, [it] was unfit for human occupancy."[4]

In 1746 the Assembly rebuilt the powder magazine, this time closer to the center of the property. They also constructed new military barracks on the magazine's original northwest-corner site. When the city fell to the British army in 1780, Charlestonians were ordered to surrender their weapons, which were to be collected and stored within the magazine. Historian Christine Trebellas notes the British carelessly gathered "'guns, fowling pieces, rifles, muskets, pistols, all crammed to the muzzle with the remaining cartridges of their late proprietors . . . cartridge-boxes, powder-horns, all recklessly into one heap.' The result was an explosion that shook the city to its foundation. The blast destroyed the magazine, the poorhouse, the guardhouse, the barracks, and the arsenal, and killed most of the soldiers and civilians in the area. Several bodies were found hurled against the neighboring Unitarian Church on Archdale Street [a full block away]."[5] According to accounts found during Trebellas's research, about two hundred people were killed; six residences and a brothel were destroyed.

The poorhouse was rebuilt along the Mazyck Street (now Logan Street) side of the lot. Those deemed insane were kept separately from the poor in this new three-story building.

A district jail and workhouse for the enslaved were added in 1802–1803, as was a new asylum for the insane in 1822. Two years later, members of the Medical Society of South Carolina, founded in 1789 to "improve the Science of Medicine, promoting liberality in the Profession, and Harmony amongst the Practitioners in this City" constructed the Medical College of South Carolina, predecessor to today's Medical University of South Carolina, behind the District Jail on the block's southwest corner.[6]

In 1826 Robert Mills, generally credited with being America's first native architect, described these public institutions in his *Statistics of South Carolina*:

Lunatic Asylum—This benevolent institution was founded in 1822; the building is now ready for the reception of patients; it will contain 150, nearly all in separate rooms; the plan of the building is such as to admit of any extension, without departure from the original design.... The original act of Legislature making appropriations for a Lunatic Asylum including also an Asylum for the Deaf and Dumb. . . . The public prison is situated on Magazine Street. . . . It is a large three-story brick building with very roomy and comfortable accommodations. . . . There has been lately added to it a four-story wing building, devoted exclusively to the confinement of criminals. It is divided into solitary cells, one for each criminal, and the whole made general fire proof. A spacious court is attached. . . .Very good health is enjoyed by the prisoners. The work house, adjoining the jail is appropriated entirely to the confinement and punishment of slaves. These were formerly compelled only occasionally to work; no means then existing of employing them regularly and effectively. The last year the City Council ordered the erection of a tread-mill; this has proved a valuable appendage to the prison, and will supercede [sic] every other species of punishment there.[7]

In 1834, the city established the Old Mariners' Hospital just north of the Medical College and south of the District Jail, along Franklin Street. And finally, in 1852, the Medical Society used a bequest of $30,000 from Col. Thomas Roper, a former mayor of Charleston who had enlisted to fight for the Patriot cause when he was just sixteen years old, to build a hospital to treat the city's sick and injured "without regard to complexion, religion or nation."[8] By 1856 Roper Hospital, named for its primary benefactor and located at the corner of Queen and Logan Streets on the block's southwest corner, was admitting patients suffering from the many epidemics that plagued Charleston throughout the nineteenth century: yellow fever, cholera, typhoid fever, and smallpox.

In *A Brave Black Regiment*, author Luis Emilio quotes from a *Charleston Courier* newspaper article describing the horrors that occurred at the hospital during the Civil War:

A chief point of attraction in the city yesterday was the Yankee hospital on Queen Street, where the principal portion of the Federal wounded, negroes and white, have been conveyed. Crowds of men, women and boys congregated in front of the building to speculate on the novel scenes being enacted within, or to catch glimpses through the doorways of the long rows of maimed and groaning beings who lined the floors of the two edifices, but this was all they could see. The operations were performed in the rear of the hospital where half a dozen or more tables were constantly occupied through the day with the mutilated subjects. The wounds generally

The two remaining historic buildings on the Old Public Square are the Charleston District Jail, c. 1802, circled at left, and the Marine Hospital, c. 1833, circled at right. The Robert Mills Manor public housing project, c. 1939, can be seen at both the lower left side and lower right, abutting two sides of the parcel. Image taken after 1940. (Circles added by author.) *Library of Congress*

are of a severe character, owing to the short distance at which they were inflicted, so that amputations were almost the only operations performed. Probably not less than seventy or eighty legs and arms; were taken off yesterday, and more are to follow to-day. The writer saw eleven removed in less than an hour. Yankee blood leaks out by the bucketful.[9]

All of these public buildings were extensively damaged in the Great Earthquake of 1886, some of them destroyed. The Mariners' Hospital ceased to serve as a medical facility and instead came to house an orphanage that would cause it to become better associated with the madcap madness of America's Great Jazz Age of the Roaring 1920s. Thanks to the Jenkins Orphanage Band, the sound of music and joy could at times be heard within this historic block. Yet most of the time, not so much.

THE SUGAR HOUSE

Charleston's Old District Jail is one of the city's most gruesomely awe-inspiring tourist attractions today, especially for those who enjoy a good ghost story, such as that of Lavinia Fisher, who is said to haunt its halls. Yet few visitors ever hear much about the jail's now-demolished companion building, the workhouse—in Charleston, more popularly known as the Sugar House. A true recounting of the events that took place there are far too unsettling for most tourists' palates.

Workhouses originally developed in Europe and the West Indies, long before Charleston annexed its own onto the District Jail in 1803. They were places where corporal punishment was used as a teaching tool or reminder to anyone who needed to mend their ways. By the early nineteenth century, however, Charleston's workhouse was used almost exclusively as a place where runaway and disobedient slaves could be sent for punishment.

Unlike similar facilities elsewhere, the name "Sugar House" seems to have been unique to Charleston. Most likely it gained the nickname after an earlier workhouse burned down and enslaved inmates had to be temporarily housed in a vacated sugar warehouse on Broad Street. By the time a new workhouse had been incorporated as part of the District Jail complex in

1803, the name "Sugar House" had become a part of Charleston's lexicon. When enslaved people overstepped their boundaries, they would be brought here, as the wryly euphemistic phrase went, "for a taste of sugar" or something to that effect.[10]

Though stories abound about cruel, sadistic slave owners—and for good reason—many Charlestonians found the punishment of their enslaved workers to be a distasteful business and appreciated the convenience of leaving such unpleasantness to someone else. Drivers, the overseers charged with making sure the enslaved completed their tasks satisfactorily, also found the Sugar House a helpful resource, as they had to maintain a working relationship with the enslaved people they supervised and therefore often preferred not to be seen as the one who personally administered the harsher punishments. In addition, it was cheap and easy: For 25 cents, one could hire a city employee to administer up to twenty lashes with a whip.

Punishment methods were brutal and varied, depending on the nature of the offense. In an article published September 20, 1838, in *The Emancipator,* editor Joshua Leavitt recorded an incident as told to him by James Matthews, a runaway who endured nearly two hundred lashes over a two-week period:

> I have heard a great deal said about hell, and wicked places, but I don't think there is any worse hell than that sugar house. It's as bad a place as can be. . . . On the top of the wall, both sides of the gate, there are sharp pointed iron bars sticking up, and all along the rest of the wall are broken glass bottles. These are to keep us from climbing over. . . . Away down in the ground, under the house is a dungeon, very cold and so dark you can't tell the difference between day and night. There are six or seven long rooms, and six little cells above and six below. The room to do the whipping in is by itself. When you get in there, every way you look you can see paddles, and whips, and cowskins, and bluejays, and cat-o'-nine tails. The bluejay has two lashes, very heavy and full of knots. It is the worst thing to whip with of any thing they have. It makes a hole where it strikes, and when they have done it will be all bloody. . . . You may

hear the whip and paddle there, all hours of the day. . . . There is no stopping. As soon as one is loosened from the rope, another is ready to be put in. Some days they have so many they don't get through till late at night. . . . [T]hey once tried to make a driver out of me. I whipped so fast it did not suit Wolf so he began whipping me.[11]

After suffering such brutal treatment, Matthews recalled that his back "would be full of scabs, and they whipped them off till I bled so that my clothes were all wet. Many a night I have laid up there in the Sugar House and scratched [the scabs] off by the handful."[12]

Stocks were another simple but brutal form of torture at the Sugar House. Prisoners' legs would be pinioned within a wooden plank, their hands tied and necks fastened by a heavy chain to a beam, making it necessary to remain

Five Dollars Reward.

Ranaway from the Subscriber on Tuesday last, a NEGRO FELLOW, named SAM, of a yellow complexion, about 5 feet 10 or 11 inches high, and about 45 years of age, very plausible, and artful; a jobbing carpenter and well known in Charleston, has a wife on Johns' Island, where it is supposed he will endeavor to go. Sam formerly belonged to the estate of Humphrey Sommers, and has a brother that belongs to David Deas, esq. Charleston. The above reward will be paid on lodging him in the Work-House or delivering him at my plantation near Goose-Creek.

Archibald M'Kewn.

March 11   sluth 5

An advertisement printed in the March 11, 1809, (Charleston) *City Gazette & Daily Advertiser* offering a reward to anyone who returned the runaway Sam, either to the owner's plantation or to the Work-House. *Museum of Early Southern Decorative Arts* in an unsupported seated position to avoid choking. Although he himself was never confined to the Sugar House, William Pinckney, a former slave, confirmed that after having been confined for weeks at a time and deprived of any basic necessities, "sometimes the slaves died in [the] stocks."[13]

Yet perhaps the most dreaded punishment of all was the treadmill, a rotating paddle wheel used to grind corn, which was in use in Charleston's Sugar House by 1825. Men and women alike were forced to walk on the treadmill for eight hours a day, seven days a week, in increments of three minutes on and three minutes off. Three minutes was just enough time to keep one conscious and going, but not enough time to give one's muscles any rest. Those who were sluggish or failed to exert the necessary effort to keep the wheel spinning efficiently received blows or lashes to the back of their legs. Exhausted, many fell and were injured—occasionally even killed—in the mechanism.

After emancipation, the Sugar House was repurposed as a city hospital, a rather odd rehabilitation choice given that the building was dank, airless,

Though no images of Charleston's specific treadmill exist, this is an example of what a nineteenth century wheel looked like. As prisoners climbed the never-ending staircase, guards would apply the whip to any that seemed to be sluggish. *Encyclopedia Britannica*

and open, with no place where those suffering contagious disease could be isolated from other patients. The white populace avoided the hospital whenever possible, and most of its patients were indigent African Americans.

As Charlestonians' world began to shake apart around 9:50 p.m. during the Great Earthquake of August 31, 1886, two of the hospital's 125 patients were killed immediately by falling debris. According to news accounts, the hospital's doors and shutters were used as stretchers to move injured patients to safety, noting: "They present a terrible spectacle. At the Hospital was also the body of a colored man, who was killed by a falling piazza, and the body of Mr. Robert Alexander, the young English analytical chemist, was . . . horribly mangled."[14]

The Sugar House was heavily damaged in the quake, as was its neighbor, the District Jail, which permanently lost its ventilation tower and fourth floor. Though the jail was repaired, the Sugar House was razed shortly afterward, and the space where so many atrocities took place today remains a mostly vacant and rarely interpreted parking lot. No sign or marker recalls the horrific history that took place there.

THE CHARLESTON DISTRICT JAIL

Located immediately west of the Sugar House on Magazine Street was Charleston's Old District Jail. In the 136 years between 1803 and 1939, it housed some of the city's most notorious murderers and malefactors, as well as the enslaved and Union prisoners of war. Local tour guides who tout the Old Jail as the city's most haunted building make a strong argument for that claim, for thousands have died within these walls.[15] From 2003 to 2020, a local tour company conducted both day and evening ghost tours through the Old Jail, and in return contributed a portion of their ticket sales toward its stabilization. Though perhaps the ghost of Lavinia Fisher is the most popular specter to roam its halls, others claim to have heard voices and slamming cell doors and felt unexplainable "cold spots" throughout the building. Their stories have been chronicled on such television networks and series as the Travel Channel, Food Network, *BuzzFeed Unsolved, Ghost Hunters*, and *Paranormal State*.

Yet despite the jail's popularity as a tourist destination in recent years, local preservationists generally agree that the Old District Jail is the most historically significant site in the city to not have benefitted from a comprehensive restoration or rehabilitation plan, though there always seems be a discussion about its future use and preservation "in the works" through one public/private partnership or another.

Contrary to its popular moniker, "The Old City Jail,"[16] this building never actually operated as a municipal prison. Rather, it was built to serve as the state's first officially designated jail. During Charles Town's colonial era, there was no prison building as we think of them today. As in the case of pirate Stede Bonnet, discussed in an earlier chapter, those who were being held over for trial were most often housed in the residence of the city marshal or other city officials, although by 1711 a "watch house" had been established within the defensive fort that sat atop Half Moon Battery (today the eastern terminus of Broad Street). That building was remodeled and expanded 1767–1769 to become what we know today as the Old Exchange Building. Visitors still enjoy hearing stories about Revolutionary War prisoners, both British and American, housed within its Provost's Dungeon. Around that same time, a new watch house was built on the southwest corner of Meeting and Broad Streets, but it was mostly used as a headquarters for Charles Town's city militia, the first paid, professionally trained police force in America.

Construction began in 1802 on the earliest part of the building that stands at 21 Magazine Street today. To add to its morbid history, it was built over what had been a public cemetery, what is commonly known as a potter's field, as described in the essay above. The original one-story brick structure was a simple rectangular design with no ornamentation, measuring just one hundred by fifty feet.[17] Accepting its first inmates in early 1803, the jail had the capacity to hold 130 malefactors, though at times, some historians have estimated, it held more than 500.

This humble original footprint was expanded in 1822 with the addition of a perpendicular four-story wing designed by Robert Mills, a Charlestonian popularly known as America's first native architect.[18] Most of Mills's wing was demolished in 1855, however, when a four-story octagonal wing designed by Charleston architects John H. Seyle and Louis J. Barbot in the gothic Romanesque Revival style replaced much of it.

At the same time, a dramatic arched doorway flanked by two crenellated towers was added to the facade, giving the building the grim, imposing aesthetic still evident today. This threatening appearance was not designed by accident. The dark, intimidating appearance of the District Jail was meant to strike fear into the heart of anyone, particularly the enslaved, who might be contemplating rebellion or other disobedience.

Along with its Romanesque Revival architectural features, a two-story ventilation tower was added atop the four-story rear wing. (At the risk of understatement, crowded prison cells can get deathly hot during Charleston's subtropical summers.) Still, the barred windows did not provide enough air to keep out the heat, nor the cold in winter. Although in his 1826 *Statistics of South Carolina*, Robert Mills noted that the recently renovated jail had "very roomy and comfortable accommodations" and that "[v]ery good health is

The Charleston District Jail as it appeared after the addition of its 1856 Romanesque Revival detailing, front door arch, and side towers.[19] *Library of Congress*

enjoyed by the prisoners,"[20] the reality is that throughout its existence, the building has served as a mecca for all kinds of vermin, disease-carrying mosquitoes and rats included. This should hardly be surprising, as part of the public square's plat was infill from a small creek.

Also during most of its time actively serving as a prison, it had no running water. Straw or wood chips served as both bedding and toilet areas. Filth was unavoidable. Though far more deaths here were actually attributable to the heat, overcrowded conditions, meager nutrition, and rampant disease that defined life—and death—in the Old District Jail, the prison's most famous tales involve inmate violence and executions, many of which were staged in the jail yard. Whippings, beatings, inmate fights, and sexual assaults were all common occurrences.

This image taken after the jail closed in 1939 shows the first-floor kitchen area, where the warden's wife and family would prepare meals for the inmates. A dumbwaiter can be seen in the center of the image, along with examples of the heavy metal bars that enclosed all window and door openings of the building. *Library of Congress*

The Old Jail housed prisoners from murderers to petty thieves, debtors to prostitutes, and prisoners of war. For much of that history, prisoners were housed according to their social status, gender, and the

This photograph captures an image of the second-floor hallway, where nonviolent criminals such as prostitutes and debtors were housed. *Library of Congress*

Though there is no documentation of which window John and Lavinia Fisher used in their failed escape plan, this window from Holding Cell #3 on the third floor would fit the profile of where the infamous couple was held in the jail's most secure ward. *Library of Congress*

Holding cells such as this on the third floor were very large rooms that held many prisoners at once. Prisoners that needed to be segregated from the rest of the inmate population could be so by bringing in metal cages, similar to a dog kennel. In this image, notice in each corner small coal-burning fireplaces that were used to heat the entire area in what was a rather ineffective effort. *Library of Congress*

nature of their crimes. The first floor housed a somewhat better class of "gentlemen" prisoners, as well as the jailer's family, all of whom worked to support the jail's functions. The warden's wife generally served as the facility's cook, nurse, and matron for female prisoners, along with assistance from their children.

Prostitutes and debtors generally were housed on the second floor, while African-American inmates and the most violent criminals, such as murderers and armed robbers, were housed on the upper two floors.

Hangings at the Charleston District Jail were staged a bit differently than those at most other places. At Charleston's Old Jail, prisoners stood in the jail yard not on a scaffolding or stage of any sort, but simply on the ground with the noose tied around their neck. The rope ran up through a tall pole on a pulley system, then back down again to the ground, where it was tied to a heavy sack. Next to the sack was a large hole. The sack was then pushed into the hole and the resulting tension would jerk the rope, and its prisoner, up high. The rationale for using this method was considered a humane one, as the chances of the prisoner's neck being snapped instantly were more likely this way—a swifter death than strangling over the course of several minutes or, in the case of poorly managed executions, even a while longer.

In addition to John and Lavinia Fisher, the jail housed a number of other high-profile inmates, perhaps most notably Denmark Vesey and the men who were accused and executed along with him on July 2, 1822, following their conviction of plotting a slave rebellion.[21] Because city officials were concerned a riot might ensue at the men's execution, they were quietly taken from the District Jail between 6:00 and 8:00 a.m. and driven at least two miles out of town for their hangings. By the end of August, another 131 slaves and free Black people had also been arrested for their connections to the conspiracy and incarcerated in the District Jail.[22] Thirty of them were released without a trial, and two died while in custody before they could be tried. Of the 101 Black people who were tried, twenty-three were acquitted and three were found not guilty but sent to the Sugar House to be whipped anyway. Vesey's daughter Sandy and thirty-six others were found guilty and sent to Cuba to be sold there. One, the Reverend Morris Brown, pastor of the AME Church, was allowed to go to Philadelphia, with the understanding that he could be arrested if he ever returned to South Carolina. His church was razed. The remaining thirty-five Black prisoners were found guilty and hanged. Four white men who were convicted of being involved in the plot were found guilty, but not executed.

One of the numerous consequences of the purported Slave Rebellion of 1822 was a new state law that required any Black sailor, free or enslaved, to remain on his ship while in port. City leaders were concerned that Black sailors would bring in news of other slave rebellions around the Atlantic or Caribbean, contributing to local tensions that continued to build throughout the first half of the nineteenth century. Black sailors who came ashore and were captured, regardless of whether any wrongdoing was involved, were incarcerated in the Old Jail and released only if "redeemed" by their captain for a fee. If the captain did not pay the fine for the return of his sailors by the time their ship had sailed, leaving them behind, they would be sold into slavery.

Two other early nineteenth-century inmates who gained fame during their stays at the Old District Jail were Jacque Alexander Tardy and John Gibson, the latter a cook who served aboard a passenger ship named the *Maria*. Tardy was born in France in 1767. As a young man, he fled with his family during the French Revolution to Saint-Domingue (Haiti), where his family acquired some wealth living on a sugar plantation. The Tardys were again displaced during the Haitian Slave Rebellion of 1791, ending up in Philadelphia, where Jacque, now using the name John, learned the tinsmithing trade.

An 1806 advertisement in a Charleston newspaper shows that Tardy had opened his own tinsmithing shop at 131 Church Street.[23] On June 16, 1809, his shop caught fire, destroying not only his house but that of his neighbors as well. With the $800 insurance settlement he received from the fire, he moved to Augusta, Georgia, for a new start in the tinsmithing business. He later accepted a position in the US Navy aboard the USS *Congress* as a captain's steward. It was not long before he was returned to his homeport of Norfolk, Virginia, and flogged for stealing from his captain's cabin then trying to sell the purloined items to his fellow crewmen. He was also later suspected, though never convicted, of poisoning his captain, who died under suspicious circumstances at the age of thirty-five.

In 1814 Tardy accepted an apprenticeship's position with a Boston dentist, who soon fired him for being "more interested in the application of various medications, than dentistry."[24] He spent the next three years doing hard labor in Boston's Charlestown State Prison for a theft conviction.

Upon his release, Tardy hopped aboard the *Maria*, bound again for Charleston. Along the route he poisoned the ship's captain and seven others by putting arsenic in their breakfast hash. Claiming to be a doctor, he prescribed doses of castor oil; of course the crewmen died anyway. He then accused the ship's cook, John Gibson, of being responsible for the poisoning. Upon the *Maria*'s arrival in Charleston, Gibson was arrested and held at the District Jail before being tried and hanged for murder on March 4, 1817, proclaiming his innocence to the end. It is likely that he was both executed and buried in the potter's cemetery there on-site.

Following Gibson's execution, Tardy returned to Philadelphia. Within a year of his arrival, he was charged and convicted of poisoning several more people aboard the *Regulator*, again blaming the ship's cook. This time the story did not fly, as the cook's good reputation was well known by his captain and others. Tardy was convicted of the crime and spent another seven years at hard labor in the Philadelphia area.

Upon his release, he headed back to Charleston, where he began advertising his services as a dentist. On November 18, 1825, Tardy attempted to steal a harbor pilot's boat named the *Cora* from its dock along the city's waterfront, enlisting the aid of two of its crewmen. All three were caught red-handed in the process. In an unsuccessful attempt to escape, Tardy fired several shots at his captors. He awaited his trial in the Charleston District Jail and, on March 3, 1826, was convicted of conspiracy to steal the boat. He was sentenced to two years in the same prison where poor John Gibson had been held and executed eight years earlier.

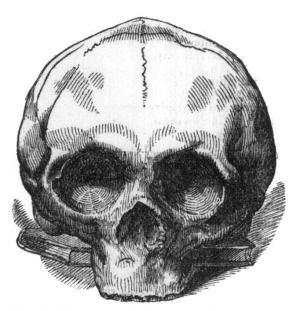

A sketch of Jacque Alexander Tardy's skull, which ran in the *Phrenological Journal and Miscellany*, vol. V, May 1828–April 1829. *WikiMedia Commons*

After his release from Charleston's District Jail, Tardy continued a life of crime, theft, and murder. Two years later, he committed suicide by slitting his own throat as the authorities, this time back in Norfolk, were once again closing in on him for again trying to steal a boat. On August 1, 1827, Dr. Brereton of the Washington Phrenological Society requested, and was given, Tardy's skull for study.

Never was the District Jail more crowded than during the American Civil War. Charleston's first Union prisoners were held at Castle Pinckney, a small island set between Charleston's docks along the Cooper River and Mount Pleasant, which had been repurposed as a POW camp soon after the war's first shots were fired just downriver at Fort Sumter. Its first captives arrived in September 1861—men who, according to a Richmond, Virginia, newspaper, included prisoners "who had evinced the most insolent and insubordinate disposition."[25] Nevertheless, life at Castle Pinckney never yielded the horror stories of other camps, such as the Washington Race Course described earlier. Because Castle Pinckney was a small island, prisoners were allowed to wander freely during the day, returning to their cells at night. Contemporary photographs suggest that prisoners and their captors even shared a sense of humor and civility toward one another.

The number of prisoners held at Castle Pinckney quickly outgrew the island's facilities, and they were transferred to the District Jail in September 1861. Hundreds of soldiers, both Union POWs and Confederate deserters, would pass through the Old Jail's arched doorway over the next four years. Even the jail yard was packed with as many tents as possible to house everyone, yet even then the facility was packed beyond capacity and prisoners had to take turns sleeping. Some days rations came down to just a handful of crackers. Still, nearly everyone in Charleston was starving during the worst parts of its siege—prisoners, guards, and populace alike.

Everything in Charleston changed on December 11, 1861, when the largest fire in the city's history swept from the northeast corner of East Bay and Hasell Streets down and across the peninsula to the western terminus of Tradd Street and the Ashley River. As the conflagration, flowing with the strong winds that roared through the city that night, took a northwesterly turn near Meeting and Broad Streets, it looked as if the jail lay right in its path.

Prisoners of the 69th New York Infantry, captured at the Battle of Bull Run, are seen lounging on Castle Pinckney in August 1861 in front of Barracks No. 7, which they humorously nicknamed "The Musical Hall, 444 Broadway," as seen on the sign above its doorway. The following month they would be moved to the overcrowded Old District Jail. *Library of Congress*

Nearly all of the prisoners were hurried upstairs and packed into one of the largest cells on the fourth floor as their Confederate guards left their posts to assist the city's firefighters in battling the flames.[26] Panicked, inmates who could squeezed through a small window opening and dropped to the ground below, many sustaining injuries in the fall. Once on the ground, however, those who jumped did not scatter to escape but stayed together and waited in an orderly fashion amid the chaos that surrounded them.

Thanks to the providence of the shifting winds, the jail did not catch fire that evening, as did nearly one-third of the city's commercial and residential structures, though it did come frighteningly close. The next morning, as the smoke and dust began to clear, the Confederate guards returned to the jail, appreciative of finding their Union captives just outside the jail awaiting their return. Afterward, they returned to Castle Pinckney for several weeks while the District Jail guards helped clean up and secure the city once again after the disastrous fire. By January all POWs were again moved back to the District Jail, which continued to serve as a POW camp until the city fell to Union troops in February 1865.

At approximately 9:50 p.m. the evening of August 31, 1886, Charlestonians' world once again was forever changed when the largest earthquake to ever hit the East Coast struck, its epicenter near Middleton Place plantation, about ten miles northwest of downtown. Virtually every building in the Charleston area was damaged in what historians now estimate must have registered between a 7.2 and a 7.4 rating on today's Richter scale. The District Jail lost, permanently, its entire fourth floor and ventilation tower, fallen into rubble. Much of the twenty-foot wall that had enclosed the Civil War prison camp also toppled and was later replaced by a lower, more modest wall. As noted earlier, the adjoining Sugar House, which by that time had been converted to a public hospital, was demolished as a result of the earthquake's damage.

Yet despite the damage, three floors of Charleston's Old District Jail still stood and continued to house prisoners for the next five decades. In 1911 Daniel Duncan, convicted of murder, was the last inmate to be executed by the jail yard's unusual hanging mechanism.

As other more modern prisons opened up around the state during the early twentieth century, to say the now-antiquated jail's structure continued to deteriorate after the earthquake is to simply state the obvious. In the 1930s the city began seeking a location on which to create new low-income public housing, and as they did, their sights turned to the old public square. Bricks that lay abandoned after the earthquake's destruction of the jail's ventilation tower, fourth floor, and surrounding wall were gathered up and used in the construction of the new housing project just beyond the jail's northern and western perimeters along Magazine and Franklin Streets. Plans were made to create a new playground out of the old jail yard, where so many executions had taken place, paupers been buried, and starving prisoners of war packed together—though that plan (dare we say fortunately?) was never fully realized.

The jail was decommissioned and its last inmates exited the building on September 13, 1939. It sat empty, unused, and deteriorating over the next sixty-one years under the ownership of the Housing Authority of

Charleston. Attempts to create an on-site museum were unsuccessful in the late 1960s and early 1970s. Though well intentioned, in hindsight, many of the incorrectly made repairs to shore up the building's structure after the earthquake did more harm than good.

It wasn't until 2000 that the future began to look brighter for the Old District Jail, when it was purchased through a complex land swap with the city by the American College of the Building Arts. The origins of this unique college began during the 1990s, following the city's devastation by Hurricane Hugo on September 21/22, 1989. In the Category 4 storm's aftermath, many owners and stewards of Charleston's historic civic buildings and residences were surprised to discover that they could not find highly skilled craftspeople in the traditional building trades—such as plaster, stone carving, wood and blacksmithing—to repair and restore their properties. Many had to look as far as Europe to find and hire qualified craftspeople with the traditional skills needed to repair their historic properties.

Created to resolve this educational gap in America, the American College of the Building Arts (ACBA) seemed the perfect fit as the next tenants and stewards of the badly deteriorating jail, seeing it as a living classroom for the skills they were learning. Among their restoration efforts was the construction of steel towers inside the building's main cellblocks, the oldest portion of the building still in existence. The towers were then bolted to the surrounding walls to slow the deterioration of the structure's masonry.

ACBA spent the next seventeen years stabilizing the jail's structural integrity. As its student enrollment increased, however, the young school began to outgrow the jail's footprint. Heating, cooling, and technology were also problems for the campus, as the jail's feet-thick masonry walls were hardly conducive to speedy internet connections, hard-wiring, re-piping, etc. In 2016 ACBA moved to its new campus in the city's rehabilitated Old Trolley Barn, c. 1897, on upper Meeting Street, and a new commercial venture began exploring ways to rehabilitate the Old District Jail into office space, preserving as much of its original historic fabric as possible. It remains to be seen how many of the building's new occupants will feel comfortable working late into the evening hours when necessary. Until then, the Charleston District Jail remains the largest unrestored property in the city's historic district.

THE OLD MARINE HOSPITAL

On July 16, 1798, America's second president, John Adams, signed into law an act to establish a series of hospitals strategically located in the East Coast port cities, designed specifically to care for sick, injured, and disabled mariners aboard both American and foreign ships in port.[27] The act stipulated that the hospitals would be funded through the deduction of 20 cents per month from each seaman's wages, a requirement some scholars consider to be America's first nationally mandated health insurance program.

Native Charlestonian and architect Robert Mills, who by the 1830s was working in Boston, was selected to design the Marine Hospital to be built in his hometown on Franklin Street between the District Jail and Medical Society of South Carolina's headquarters. In doing so, Mills contributed the first example of the Gothic Revival style to the city's rich architectural continuum, with the two-story hospital featuring lancet arches and quatrefoil-shaped columns supporting double-story piazzas.[28] The piazzas' railings also followed a medieval motif, perhaps an eerie nod to the looming Romanesque Revival behemoth to its north.

Like so many other historic buildings in Charleston, the Old Marine Hospital has been used for many purposes since its construction was completed in 1834. For a while the Medical Society used it as a teaching hospital; during the Civil War it became a military hospital. After the war, a small group of Episcopal women opened a free school for Black children here until 1870.[29] In the latter half of the twentieth century, it became a library and administrative offices for the Housing Authority of Charleston. Yet it was in the final years of the nineteenth century and early decades of the twentieth, 1895–1937, that the old hospital came alive as the home for a group of orphans who would lead the nation into what we remember as the splendorous Jazz Age of the Roaring 1920s.

Daniel Jenkins had been born a slave on a Barnwell County farm before the Civil War. As a young man in his twenties, he left his rural home to seek his fortunes in Charleston.[30] Soon he fell in love and married Lena James. He found a job delivering lumber and moonlighted as pastor of the New Tabernacle Fourth Baptist Church. It was several years later, however, as he delivered lumber to the railroad station one bitterly cold December day in

Image of the Marine Hospital (aka Jenkins Orphanage), featuring Gothic Revival details; taken in 1934, shortly before the Reverend Jenkins died and the orphanage moved to new quarters in North Charleston. The Old District Jail can be seen at left. *Library of Congress*

1891, that the Reverend Jenkins realized his true calling when he came upon four starving orphans huddled in a boxcar trying to keep one another warm.

Though the Jenkinses struggled financially to keep themselves and their own children fed, they took in the homeless boys, asking their church's congregation to pitch in as much as they could afford, which unfortunately wasn't a lot. Soon they were not only caring for these four children but also for dozens of others who could not find a haven within the state's nine orphanages, all of which had been established for white children only.

Thus began Jenkins Orphanage. Within two years, Daniel and Lena Jenkins were caring for 360 orphaned children. Within two more years, nearly five hundred children were sheltering together in a shed on upper King Street. Jenkins affectionately called the children his "little black lambs."

In January 1892, Jenkins sought permission from the city to use the Marine Hospital, which had been sitting empty since the free school closed twenty years earlier, to house the children. In his request, Jenkins noted its ideal location in the shadow of the Old District Jail and Work House, where enslaved people were once punished for disobedience and waywardness: a constant reminder, Jenkins said, to his orphaned charges of what could happen to little children who strayed from the straight-and-narrow path of righteousness.

The donations Jenkins received from his congregation, even when augmented by a small stipend from the city, still weren't enough to keep the children adequately fed, clothed, and educated. Though a religious man, the Reverend Jenkins placed little faith in charity and wanted the children to understand that they had to make their own way in the world without

The Reverend Daniel Jenkins, founder of the Jenkins Orphanage. *The Jenkins Institute*

counting on help from others. He insisted that the orphanage sustain itself through earned income. And he had an idea of just how they might do that.

Though people were hesitant about donating money to the orphanage, most seemed amenable to donating old musical instruments. Likewise, Citadel students willingly parted with any military uniforms they had outgrown or were ready to discard. With that, and the help of two talented young musicians who were willing to teach something they loved for little more than their room and board in return, Jenkins's "little black lambs" were poised to usher in America's next cultural phenomenon.

Soon the children were not only learning to read music but also how to play all of the donated instruments. Oboes, drums, horns, cymbals—each child was taught to play them all rather than specialize in one. Though his medical information was incorrect, Jenkins believed, and told *Time* magazine in a 1935 interview, that wind instruments helped the children stave off tuberculosis.

The orphanage's bands soon became a fixture on many Charleston street corners. They brought an energy, enthusiasm, and spark with fast-paced syncopated rhythms and irresistible dance moves, unlike anything Charlestonians had ever seen before. After every performance, Jenkins asked for donations by literally passing his hat among the crowd. His plan worked. Soon five of the Jenkins Orphanage Bands were playing for audiences all along the East Coast, as well as at the St. Louis World Fair and Anglo-American Exposition. The band even toured London, giving a command performance for King George V. In 1905 they led President Theodore Roosevelt's inaugural parade, as they did again for President William Howard Taft four years later.

Perhaps the most defining icon of the Roaring Twenties in America was a new dance craze called the Charleston, whose origins can be traced to Jenkins's charges and their street performances in the Holy City. Former orphan and band member, Russell Brown, introduced the band's free-spirited steps at a popular nightclub called The Jungle in Harlem, New York, which he frequented as an adult.[31] A longshoreman by day, Brown was a popular regular at the club where, because of his rich Gullah accent, he acquired the nickname "Charleston." Fellow patrons, some of whom were also transplanted

The Jenkins Orphanage Band would work their way through a city, playing a musical set on one block before moving several blocks away to repeat their performance. After each performance, the Reverend Jenkins would pass his hat for donations. Their upbeat, syncopated quickstep style would help usher in America's great Jazz Age. *The Jenkins Institute*

dock workers from South Carolina, would urge Brown to perform his signature quickstep on the dance floor, calling out "Hey, Charleston, do your dance!" Others quickly adopted the dance's vibrant steps and began referring to it as "doing the Charleston."

James P. Johnson, one of the club's regular pianists, who also worked occasionally with Broadway shows, composed several versions of a tune that complemented the quickstep beat Brown used. Johnson then introduced one of the tunes, along with the dance, in an off-Broadway musical titled *Running Wild* that opened on October 29, 1923.[32] A two-act comedy about the adventures of two likable scamps and billed as "the World's greatest all black entertainment," the show featured a song titled "Old Fashioned Love," which went on to become the tune most often associated with the dance.

Jazz legend Josephine Baker dances the Charleston at
Folies Bergère, Paris, 1926. *WikiMedia Commons*

Part of the appeal of the new dance was that it could be performed
alone, with a partner, or in a group similar to more recent line dance versions
of the Electric Slide or Macarena. One thing that was definitely required,
however, was the ability to move one's legs and arms—indeed all of one's
body parts!—in a free, uninhibited manner, an ability that meshed well with
the short, sassy, sleeveless flapper dresses that characterized the decade's fashion trends.

Yet fashion always changes. By the 1930s, trends in ladies' semiformal
attire had begun to revert once again to floor-length gowns, just one of the
factors that probably contributed to the dance's decline in popularity—you
can't do the Charleston unless scandalously clad in the skimpy shifts that
keep your knees and elbows free to fling.

The new decade of the 1930s brought other changes as well. The Reverend Jenkins died in 1937, about the time the Old Marine Hospital was damaged in a fire that destroyed two long wings on the building's eastern side. Only about half the original hospital was deemed salvageable, too small a space to house the orphanage. The children were relocated to a new site in North Charleston, and the Housing Authority of Charleston absorbed the old hospital as part of the new Robert Mills Manor public housing project they were beginning to build around the old public square.

The orphanage's bands continued to play for about another decade. By the 1950s, however, new public subsidies began to eliminate the need for the children to earn their own living—a change in public policy that ironically ran contrary to Jenkins's personal philosophy of learning to fend for oneself. By the mid-1950s, rock and roll had taken over as the new musical genre,

A group of flappers "doin' the Charleston" with the Jenkins Orphanage Band in front of the Old Marine Hospital, 1920s. *The Jenkins Institute*

and the Jenkins Orphanage Bands, like the Roaring Twenties in which they had come to international prominence, slipped quietly into history.

Today, Charleston's Marine Hospital is one of only eight antebellum hospitals built under the 1798 Act for the Relief of Sick and Disabled Seamen still in existence. Like the Old District Jail, it is listed on the National Register of Historic Places. Though never reaching its former popularity, the Charleston is still danced by people around the world who enjoy performing its exuberant dance steps, popularized by the Jenkins Orphanage Bands and which defined the spirit of the Roaring Twenties.

PART VI
CURSE OF THE BRACKISH WATER

THE DRIEST PLACE
ON EARTH

One of the hedonistic pleasures Charlestonians have embraced from the moment the first permanent settlers aboard the *Carolina* stepped ashore in April 1670 has been their love of alcohol. Ship's captain Joseph West complained that some of the early settlers "were so much addicted to Rum that they will do little but whilst the bottle is at their nose."[1] Historian Walter J. Fraser Jr. was generous enough to suggest that this may at least partially have been attributable to the taste of the port town's drinking water, noting that at least one early letter-writer claimed the "Water about Town to be so Brackish that it is scarcely potable unless mixed with . . . Liquors."[2]

Like other port cities, Charles Town's streets were full of itinerant mariners and traders with time and money on their hands. Things were getting so out of control that by 1672, just two years after the colony's founding, the Grand Council censured merchants who sold "strong drink" and contributed to "drunkenness, idleness, and quarrelling."[3] Henceforth, the Council declared, anybody selling liquor or beer must be licensed to do so. Regardless of this act, settlers, sailors, traders, and the indigenous population could often be found in taverns such as the Bowling Green House, Dillon's, or Shepherd's Tavern, "tyed by the Lipps to a pewter engine of beer, cider, rum, punch, brandy or Madeira wine. These 'sparkes,' as one who knew them well remarked, thought 'little of drinking 15 or 16 pounds[worth] at one Bout.'"[4]

Soon after the colony's resettlement on the peninsula in 1680, the Assembly passed another act calling for "the suppression of Idle, Drunken and Swearing Persons," later amending the act to prohibit anyone from entering "punch houses, or tippling houses, during the time of Divine Service."[5] An early female writer bemoaned the fact that Charleston's men "impaire their health by the intemperate use of spirituous liquors, and keeping late hours."[6]

One can't help but wonder, was it a coincidence that for most of the colonial period, Charles Town's governing bodies met in the "long rooms" located above their favorite taverns? If so, did worried wives have just cause to criticize their unsteady husbands when they arrived home late smelling of alcohol, since they were simply doing their civic duty by attending council meetings? Still, things got so bad that even some council members were removed from office because of their excessive public displays of "frequent drunkenness and scandalous behavior."[7]

Eventually, things in Charles Town became so raucous that local leaders desperately petitioned the Lords Proprietors to send them both a good physician and a "Godly and orthodox" minister.[8] Unfortunately, one of the first Anglican priests the Proprietors sent, the Reverend Atkin Williamson who served St. Philip's Church, was soon sent back to England for baptizing a bear while under the influence of a spirituous substance.

With the first shots fired upon Fort Sumter in 1861, Charlestonians made it clear they felt no obligation to comply with burdensome governmental mandates that threatened their way of life and the pleasures they held dear. After all, throughout most of the eighteenth and early nineteenth centuries, Charleston had served as America's most cosmopolitan Atlantic seaport, setting the colonial standard for style and fashion while cultivating and supplying much of the world's demand, first, for rice and indigo and later for its coveted long-staple cotton.

Indeed, by then Charlestonians had already invested two centuries in creating an aristocratic tradition that held themselves in the highest regard, elevated enough to become the first to secede from a central federal government they felt was unduly burdening them with mandates, taxes, and regulations, taking it upon themselves to fire the opening salvo that began the most horrific war in American history.

Even after the losses of the American Civil War, this feeling of hereditary superiority continued, leading Charlestonians to generally consider themselves above the laws and social mores that governed lesser souls, even those within their own state. Small wonder, then, that the city's leaders and citizens scoffed at the idea that they would ever submit to the demands of a boorish Upstate governor who was determined, decades before federal passage of the Volstead Act in 1920, to make Charleston "the driest place on Earth."[9]

THE RISE OF PITCHFORK
BEN TILLMAN

Benjamin Ryan Tillman Jr. came bawling into the world on August 11, 1847, the last of eleven children born to Benjamin Sr. and Sophia Hancock Tillman on the family farm in Edgefield County, a rural community about midway up the state's western edge. Though only about 150 miles from Charleston as the crow flies, the two places in many ways were entirely different worlds, particularly during the second half of the nineteenth century. Owning about twenty-five hundred acres and eighty-six enslaved laborers, the Tillmans were among the largest landowners in the Edgefield District along the state's border with Georgia, a violent region even when measured against the standards of rural antebellum South Carolina.[1]

Yet even within this context, the Tillman family seemed to have a particular penchant for finding trouble. Ben Sr., who died just two years after Ben Jr.'s birth, was known to have killed at least one man and had served time after being convicted of rioting. One of Ben Jr.'s brothers was killed in a duel and another in a "domestic dispute." One died in the Mexican-American War and another as the result of wounds he sustained in the Civil War. A fifth died at the age of fifteen of unknown causes.

Clearly, Ben's most colorful sibling was his oldest brother, George. Born in 1826 and therefore twenty-one years older than Ben, George was an attorney who had been convicted of killing a man who accused him of cheating in a card game. Apparently one not easily deterred, George continued his flourishing law practice from his jail cell as he served the resulting two-year sentence for manslaughter.[2] He even ran and was successfully elected to the

South Carolina State Senate while still incarcerated. George would go on to represent South Carolina in the US House of Representatives as well. The family tradition continued when George's son James H. Tillman, while serving as the state's lieutenant governor in 1903, fatally shot Narciso Gener Gonzales, a founding editor of Columbia's *The State* newspaper, during a public confrontation on the front steps of the South Carolina State House. The Tillmans were a rough family.

As the Civil War began, young Ben left home to attend Bethany, a nearby secondary boarding school. He returned home in 1863 to help his mother, who was experiencing financial difficulties during the war years, then reenrolled at Bethany the following semester. In June 1864, sixteen-year-old Ben dropped out of Bethany for good to enlist in the Confederate army. Before he could join his unit, however, he fell seriously ill, having developed a brain tumor that ultimately resulted in the loss of his left eye. By the time Ben had recovered, the war was lost and the Tillmans, along with the rest of the state, were impoverished.

South Carolina governor Benjamin Ryan Tillman lost his left eye to a brain tumor when he was in his teens. *WikiMedia Commons*

Ben took over stewardship of the Tillmans' farm, where his family's former slaves, now freedmen, toiled in the same fields—living, working, and suffering in ways not much different than they had done during their days of enslavement. The fact that some chose, now legally, to leave the plantation in search of a new, better life infuriated Ben Tillman, who continued to treat his workers as if they were still enslaved, applying the whip whenever he felt it necessary "to drive the slovenly Negroes to work."[3]

As the state transitioned from its Reconstruction-era governance and Federal troops returned to their Northern homes for good in the latter half of the 1870s, Tillman became increasingly involved in local political activities. He was an ardent supporter of the Red Shirts, a white supremacist paramilitary group that sought to suppress Black voting rights through violence and intimidation during the 1876 election, at which time Tillman was the largest agrarian landowner in the Edgefield District.

At the risk of giving short shrift to the many defining characteristics of Tillman's lasting legacy and impact on the cultural soul and racial history of South Carolina,[4] suffice it to say that by the 1880s, he had defined himself as the champion of South Carolina's white male farmers, fighting against the Lowcountry's lawyers, politicians, merchants, and plantation aristocrats. He denounced the old Charleston guard, who for so long had held the power in the state's leadership, as a ring of "broken-down politicians and old superannuated Bourbon aristocrats who are thoroughly incompetent, who worship the past, and are incapable of progress of any sort, but who boldly assume to govern us by Divine Right."[5]

Tillman espoused that Charleston's long-dominant aristocratic conservatives were holding back the rest of the state's agricultural interests and progress, and cast the issues facing the state as Charleston versus everyone else. "Charleston's influence had aroused envy, and it was not hard to convert it into popular suspicion and wrath," *Post and Courier* columnist Brian Hicks quotes from William Watts Ball's book *The State That Forgot*. "The political leaders of that day inflamed the people to look upon Charleston as the hatchery of their woes, imagined or real."[6]

In an 1890 gubernatorial election speech on the steps of Charleston City Hall, Tillman railed: "You Charleston people are a peculiar people . . .

you are the most arrogant set of cowards that ever drew the free air of heaven. . . . You are the most self-idolatrous people in the world. I want to tell you that the sun doesn't rise and set in Charleston,"[7] and with that he committed himself to the city's demise. He even went so far as to call The Citadel, South Carolina's revered military college which was based in Charleston, a "dude factory."

Tillman eventually earned the nickname "Pitchfork Ben," not only because of his agrarian roots and political platform, but also because in 1896—a time when he was being considered by some as a possible presidential candidate for the Democratic Party—he delivered a speech critical of then-president Grover Cleveland, a man of admittedly generous proportions, threatening to prod the posterior of that big fat "bag of beef" with said farming implement.[8] After that, editorial cartoonists across the nation began depicting Tillman with a pitchfork in hand, taking jabs at his political opponents.

As he rose through the political ranks, first as governor from 1890 to 1894, then as a US senator from 1895 until his death in 1918, Tillman sought to destroy many of the things that old Charlestonians held dear— and one of the things Charlestonians had long held most dear was their liquor.

ON A POPULISTIC BASIS.

A FORECAST OF THE CONSEQUENCE OF A POPOCRATIC VICTORY TO THE SUPREME COURT OF THE UNITED STATES.

Harper's Weekly magazine (September 12, 1896) ran this editorial cartoon of what the US Supreme Court might look like if William Jennings Bryan had won that year's presidential race. Among the supposed justices are Illinois governor John Peter Altgeld (rising at center right). To his left, with pitchfork in hand, is South Carolina's US senator Ben Tillman. *WikiMedia Commons*

THE DISPENSARY
ACT OF 1893

In Charleston, drinking wasn't just a tradition, it was a way of life, an inalienable right. Yet within the larger context of the state, prohibition had become an important issue by the time Tillman ran for the governorship, fueled in part by a revivalism of Baptist and Methodist sentiments sweeping the state during the 1880s. A man who was known to imbibe himself from time to time and whose religious fervor waxed and waned with political expediency,[1] Tillman apparently didn't have any personal convictions about the evils of alcohol. Most sources agree that he did not consider absolute prohibition to be either practical or desirable.

Yet many influential members of the state's white Democratic Party did, and Tillman was committed to embracing anything that consolidated the white vote against Black Republicans' newly established civil rights. Despite one's personal affinity—or lack thereof—for Tillman's character, there was a genius to his Dispensary Act of 1893: The new law fell short of prohibiting liquor sales altogether, yet allowed the state to control its sale and profit. This approach helped appease the religiously fervent white Democrats, Tillman's party base, while offering a compromise to the smaller, but still significant, Democratic group opposed to prohibition. Through a series of complex parliamentary machinations, Governor Tillman maneuvered the state legislature into passing the Dispensary Act at 5:30 a.m. on December 24, 1892, the last day of that year's legislative session. The law went into effect July 1, 1893, the first (and last) time an attempt to create a state monopoly on alcohol sales has ever been successful in the United States.

Everybody won a little something in the deal—though no one more than Tillman himself and his state coffers, which benefited from the potential for graft within a political bureaucracy that sold alcohol. In a lengthy letter condemning the governor's move, an anonymous writer who referred to himself (or herself) only as "a Citizen of South Carolina" wrote: "The idea that the Dispensary Law was to promote temperance is a sham. The men who engineered it probably expected that it should be a money making business for the State."[2]

The new law was met with varying degrees of opposition across the state, though nowhere more so than in Charleston. Indeed, the closer a county lay geographically to Charleston, the more likely it was to oppose Tillman's Dispensary Act. Shortly after its passage, the South Carolina Supreme Court ruled the new law to be unconstitutional, asserting that the state had no right to unfairly compete with for-profit private enterprise. Again, however, through a series of well-timed judicial term expirations and backroom politics, Tillman was able to stave off a final court decision until one of his own joined the three-judge court to support his cause.[3]

Charlestonians and their law enforcement officials initially responded to Tillman's Dispensary Act simply by ignoring it. The governor countered the city's slight by supporting a political ally, John Ficken, in a successful race in Charleston's next mayoral election. Ficken replaced the leadership of Charleston's law enforcement team with another Tillman crony as the new police chief, effectively allowing the governor to take control of Charleston's police department. In addition, Tillman began sending state law enforcement officers down from Columbia to root out illegal alcohol production and consumption in the Lowcountry. Charlestonians parried that challenge by creating what appeared on the surface to be legitimate establishments that purported to be exhibition halls, but which were essentially bars illegally selling liquor. They were called Blind Tigers.

Dozens of these Blind Tiger exhibition halls opened in Charleston after passage of the Dispensary Act. For a small fee, patrons could enter the hall, have a seat, and wait a specified period of time for the appearance of a rare, tamed blind tiger that might (or might not) perform tricks. While waiting, the patron was given a "free" drink, a loophole deemed allowable under the law as long as no money for the drink itself changed hands. Should the anticipated tiger not make its appearance within the allotted time (and rarely does one come across tamed blind tigers in Charleston), the patron would repay the exhibition's "admission fee" and receive his next free drink.

Tillman was outraged by this farce, vowing that if Charlestonians would not comply with his Dispensary Act, he would make the city "dry enough to burn," sending compliance officers "to cover every city block with a man."[4] So committed was Tillman to enforcing the Dispensary Act in Charleston that he even ordered some of his law enforcement officers, all of whom were white men, to wear blackface in an attempt to root out illegal drinking within Charleston's African-American community.

Still, it hadn't been that long since Federal troops had finally left the city, and Charlestonians were in no mood to accept a new occupying force telling them what to do. And, as Tillman was about to find out, there was at least one Charleston businessman who was ready to draw a line in the sand and meet his challenge.

VINCENT CHICCO: KING
OF THE BLIND TIGERS

A Tuscan immigrant, Vincent Chicco was born in 1851 and received only a rudimentary education before leaving his Italian home as a teenager to seek his fortune in the merchant marines. His travels eventually brought him into Charleston Harbor where he decided to settle, first taking a job with the railroad then joining the local police department. Chicco took the American Oath of Allegiance in 1874, and in 1885 married a local girl and started a family.

Soon afterward, Chicco left the police force and opened a grocery store at 83/85 Market Street, in a retail space below his young family's second-floor apartment. The grocery store grew over time, offering cigar sales, a restaurant, and eventually serving alcohol. Local advertisements published before 1893 list Chicco as a saloonkeeper. After passage of the Dispensary Act, however, his business was no longer described as a saloon, though his ads continued to make it clear that wine and liquor could be purchased there.[1]

Barely two weeks after the Dispensary Act's enforcement began in July 1893, Vincent Chicco became the first Charlestonian arrested for illegally selling and serving alcohol on the premises. Yet in choosing to make an example of Chicco, a man the governor referred to as an "uneducated immigrant," Tillman had picked the wrong man.

Charlestonians' public protests on Chicco's behalf bordered on rioting. Fortunately, before things got too out of hand, Chicco was quickly tried by a friendly local judge who not only freed him immediately with the court's apologies but also charged the state law enforcement officer who arrested

Vincent Chicco's grocery store, located at 83/85 Market Street, with an image of Chicco inset at top right. *University of South Carolina, South Caroliniana Library*

him with assault. From that point on, Chicco committed himself to leading Charlestonians' fight against the Dispensary Act. Despite this arrest, and a number of subsequent ones, nothing dissuaded Chicco from continuing to sell alcohol, one way or another, through his Market Street storefront. Chicco had become Tillman's nemesis, causing the governor to refer to him as "a kind of Dago devil."[2]

Tillman and Chicco were well-matched enemies. At one point, Chicco introduced to his retail line a new brand of cigars he called "The Two Determined," fancifully boxed with a lid that featured opposing profiles of himself and Governor Tillman, surrounded by flourishes of military objects and a figure of Cupid lovingly holding a lyre.

Each time Chicco was arrested and hauled into court, he seemed to find a way to skirt the charges. He was accused of operating his Market Street grocery as a place "where people are permitted to resort for the purpose of drinking alcoholic liquors and beverages in a manner not authorized by law,"[3] and the prosecution contended that allowing him to continue doing so would cause "great injury to the public." Chicco responded to the charge by saying that while he did operate a grocery and restaurant at that address, no illegal activities were going on. The prosecution then asked about what took place above the restaurant, at 83½ Market Street, the Chiccos' residential apartment. A normalized immigrant who had studied hard to become a United States citizen, Chicco refused to answer, asserting his Fifth Amendment right against self-incrimination and stating that the 83½ Market Street address had not been included in the indictment brought against him.

Vincent Chicco so enthusiastically flaunted Tillman's dispensary laws that he created a promotional marketing "token" for his Market Street business. Though its motto innocently reads "Good for 5 cents in Trade at Chicco's Cafe," the reverse side of the token features the image of a blindfolded tiger, leaving no doubt as to the true nature of the business carried on there.[4]

Chicco's arrests and trials always made headlines in Charleston and were heavily covered by the local newspapers. Soon Vincent Chicco became a household name, a local hero, and the city's champion in standing up to the governor. The press hailed him as "King of the Blind Tigers." Chicco eventually used his newfound notoriety to go into politics himself, successfully attaining a seat on the Charleston City Council as an alderman for his ward. He won reelection five times, earning him the additional nickname of "The Mayor of Ward Three."

As many had anticipated, a state-run monopoly on alcohol sales was ripe for abuse and graft, and indeed such was the case in South Carolina. Instances of officials' siphoning off dispensary money, soliciting bribes from suppliers, and selling liquor on the sly had become so numerous that by 1904, the General Assembly passed an act allowing counties to choose for themselves whether they would allow private alcohol sales. As anticipated, many in the Upstate chose outright prohibition, while those along Charleston's coastal edge opted for local sales. By 1907, with the passage of the Carey-Cothran Law, the state's General Assembly abolished the state dispensary system.

Governor Tillman died in office in 1918 while serving as a US senator, just two years before the Volstead Act tried to enforce temperance on the national level—an effort as well received in Charleston as the state's had been more than a quarter century before. Vincent Chicco died ten years later, once again one-upping the governor, at the age of seventy-eight, having sold off the last of his businesses and living comfortably in Charleston's Ansonborough neighborhood. In writing Chicco's October 26 obituary, journalist Timmons Pettigrew noted: "The city nearly shut down for his funeral in 1928, as well it should have. The 'King of Blind Tigers' is someone we can all draw inspiration from. He was an underdog, a free spirit, an independent thinker."[5] Pettigrew characterized Chicco as "possessing a forceful personality" and being a "raconteur of ability."

Federal prohibition mandates were repealed in 1933 and Charlestonians have happily enjoyed their customary drinking habits ever since. Today the names Blind Tiger and Vincent Chicco live on only in the names of two local restaurants—their significance today largely unknown except by those patrons who, while waiting on their orders, take the time to read the entertaining little history blurbs on the back of the menus.

NOTES

PART I: THE MERRY MONARCH AND HIS HOLY CITY

1 Robert Rosen, *A Short History of Charleston* (San Francisco: Lexikos, 1982; 2nd edition Charleston, SC: Peninsula Press, 1992), 9.

2 H. L. Mencken, *A Book of Burlesques* (New York: John Lane Company, 1916). Reprinted in *The American Mercury*, vol. 4, no. 13, January 1925, 56.

3 For an interesting discussion on Puritan dress codes, see https://www.new englandhistoricalsociety.com/puritan-dress-code-and-outrage-slashed-sleeves/.

4 Henry Godfrey Roseveare, "Charles II, King of Great Britain and Ireland," in the *Encyclopedia Britannica*. Accessed at https://www.britannica.com /biography/Charles-II-king-of-Great-Britain-and-Ireland, July 10, 2021.

5 Thomas Seccombe, "Walter, Lucy," in Sidney Lee (ed.), *The Dictionary of National Biography*, 1885–1900, vol. 59 (London: Smith, Elder & Co., 1899), 259–60. Accessed at https://en.wikisource.org/wiki/Dictionary_of_National _Biography,_1885-1900/Walter,_Lucy, July 10, 2021.

6 Rosen, *A Short History of Charleston*, 9.

7 "Papers of Thomas Hearne" (November 17, 1706) quoted in C. E. Doble. (ed.), *Remarks and Collections of Thomas Hearne*, vol. 1 (Oxford: Clarendon Press for the Oxford Historical Society, 1885), 308.

8   A thorough discourse of Wilmot's verse and the king's response can be found in the forward of *The Tryal of William Penn and William Mead*, 1667. In the public domain and available for free download at https://manybooks.net/titles /anonetext05twpwm10.html.

HOW CHARLESTON EARNED ITS NAME "THE HOLY CITY"

1   Walter J. Fraser Jr., *Charleston! Charleston!* (Columbia, SC: University of South Carolina Press, 1989), 10.
2   Thomas Cooper, MD, LLD (ed.), *The Statutes at Large of South Carolina, Containing the Acts from 1682 to 1716 Inclusive*, vol. II (Columbia, SC: A. S. Johnston Publisher, 1837), 131–33.
3   For more on the Huguenots' assimilation in Carolina, see "The Cainhoy Massacre."
4   Cyrus Addler and Joseph Jacobs, "South Carolina" in the *Jewish Encyclopedia*, 12 vols., published 1901–1906. Accessed July 15, 2021; in the public domain and available for download at https://www.jewishencyclopedia.com/articles /13937-south-carolina#3206.
5   *South Carolina Council Journal*, March 3, 1753, no. 21, 298–99. Accessed at http://www.charlestonmuslims.com/?page_id=2 July 15, 2021.
6   For more on the Quakers in Charles Town, see "Mary Fisher Bailey Cross: A Woman on a Mission."
7   Fraser, 5. For more on the Goose Creek Men, see "Charles Town's Piratical Heyday."
8   Ibid., 27.

THE GAYEST, WEALTHIEST PEOPLE IN AMERICA

1   Maurice Mathews, "A Contemporary View of Carolina in 1680," found in the *South Carolina Historical Magazine* 55 (July 1954, 158).
2   "Journal of Josiah Quincy, Junior, 1773," found in the *Proceedings of the Massachusetts Historical Society* 49 (June 1916) 424–81.
3   Ibid.
4   J. Hector St. John de Crèvecoeur, *Letters from an American Farmer: Describing Certain Provincial Situations, Manners, and Customs, Not Generally Known; and Conveying Some Idea of the Late and Present Interior Circumstances of the British Colonies of North America*, 1782. Letter IX.

5   Dr. Johann Schopf, *Travels in the Confederation*, 1784. Accessed July 15, 2021; available for free download at http://livetopworld.co/3.hp?i=Travels+In+The +Confederation+%5b1783+1784%5d+From+The+German+Of+Johann +David+Schoepf+Schopf+Johann+David+1752+1800.php1&sub_id=all.

6   Samuel Pepys, 1633–1703, *The Diary of Samuel Pepys: Daily Entries from the 17th Century Diary*. Robert Lathan, William Matthews, and William A. Armstrong (eds.) (London: HarperCollins. Accessed at https://www .pepysdiary.com/encyclopedia/7371/#:~:text=Horse%20racing%2C%20 the%20favorite%20pastime%20of%20King%20Charles,Portugal.%20 She%20was%20married%20to%20Charles%20in%201662, July 17, 2021.

THE SPORT OF KINGS

1   Samuel Pepys, 1633–1703, *The Diary of Samuel Pepys: Daily Entries from the 17th Century Diary*. Robert Lathan, William Matthews, and William A. Armstrong (eds.) (London: HarperCollins). Accessed at https://www .pepysdiary.com/encyclopedia/7371/, July 17, 2021. Other sources dispute, or at least highly qualify, Pepys's claim.

2   For more on the Childsbury Race Track, see "The Chapels of Berkeley County."

3   For a more in-depth discussion on the Washington Race Course, see "The Hopes and Horrors of Hampton Park."

4   Walter J. Fraser Jr., *Charleston! Charleston!* (Columbia, SC: University of South Carolina Press, 1989), 4.

TRIPPING THE LIGHT FANTASTIC

1   Walter J. Fraser Jr., *Charleston! Charleston!* (Columbia, SC: University of South Carolina Press, 1989), 20.

2   The *South-Carolina Gazette* (Charlestown [SC]) 1732–1775, available through the Library of Congress digital collections at https://www.loc.gov/item /sn84026943/. Accessed July 1, 2021.

A LEGACY OF ILLICIT LOVE

1   Krystle Kline, *Social Evil in the Holy City: Prostitution in Charleston, SC, 1900– 1920*. Doctoral dissertation, University of Michigan, 2012, 2.

NOTES

Robert Rosen, *A Short History of Charleston* (San Francisco: Lexikos, 1982), 19.

Walter J. Fraser Jr., *Charleston! Charleston!* (Columbia, SC: University of South Carolina Press, 1989), 22.

S. M. Wynne, "Catherine [Catherine of Braganza, Catarina Henriqueta de Bragança] 1638–1705," found in the *Oxford Dictionary of National Biography* (Oxford University Press, 2004). Online edition accessed at doi:10.1093/ref:odnb/4894, July 28, 2021.

Guida Myrl Jackson Laufer, *Women Rulers throughout the Ages: An Illustrated Guide* (The Internet Archive, 1999), 83. Accessed at https://archive.org/details/isbn_9791576070917/page/83/mode/2up, July 18, 2021.

Margaret Gilmour, *The Great Lady, A Biography of Barbara Villiers, Mistress of Charles II* (Alfred A. Knopf Publishing, 1941.)

Ibid.

"Palmer, Roger of Llanfyllin Hall, Mont.," found in the *History of Parliament, British Political, Social and Local History Online*, at http://www.historyofparliamentonline.org/volume/1660-1690/member/palmer-roger-1634-1705. Accessed July 18, 2021.

George E. Cokayne, "Bastards of Charles II," found in *The Complete Peerage VI* (London: St. Catherine Press, 1926), appendix F.

Antonia Fraser, *King Charles II* (Abergavenny, Wales: Phoenix Paperbacks, 2002), 209.

R. E. Pritchard, *Scandalous Liaisons: Charles II and His Court* (United Kingdom: Amberley, 2015), 182.

Pepys. Accessed at https://www.pepysdiary.com/diary/1665/04/ on July 18, 2021.

Ibid.

Charles Beauclerk, *Nell Gwyn: Mistress to a King* (Atlantic Monthly Press, 2005). Available through The Internet Archive, https://archive.org/details/nellgwynmistress0000beau. Accessed July 18, 2021.

F. H. W. Sheppard (ed.). "Pall Mall, South Side, Past Buildings: No 79 Pall Mall: Nell Gwynne's House" in *Survey of London, Volumes 29 and 30: St. James Westminster, Part 1* (1960), 377–78. Accessed June 10, 2021 at www.british-history.ac.uk.

Charles Beauclerk, *Nell Gwyn: Mistress to a King* (London: Macmillan Publishing, 2015), 307.

Ibid.

18   Ibid., 249.

19   Eleanor Herman, *Sex with Kings: 500 Years of Adultery, Power, Rivalry, and Revenge* (New York: HarperCollins, 2005), 162.

20   Charles S. Saint-Evremond (1613–1703), *The Letters of Saint Evremond*. Translated with introduction by Rene Ternois (Paris: Didier, 1967), 146–49.

21   Herman, 188.

22   Tim Madge, *Royal Yachts of the World*, 34. Available for free download at https://archive.org/details/royalyachtsofwor0000madg.

23   Hesketh Pearson, *Charles II: His Life and Likeness* (London: Heinemann, 1960), 147.

PART II: DANCE OF THE HEMPEN JIG

CHARLES TOWN'S PIRATICAL HEYDAY

1   Nicholas Butler, PhD, "The Pirate Hunting Excursions of 1718," *Charleston Time Machine* podcast, Charleston County Public Library, November 23, 2018. Accessed at https://www.ccpl.org/charleston-time- machine/pirate -hunting-expeditions-1718, March 3, 2021.

2   The practice of privateering is not just a thing of the past, as seen in this February 28, 2022, *Fox News* feature headlined: "Republican bill would allow US citizens to seize yachts, planes of Russian oligarchs amid Ukraine invasion: Texas Rep. Lance Gooden legislation would revive use of letters of marque and reprisal" at https://www.foxnews.com/politics/gooden-americans-seize-russian -yachts-planes-oligarchs-ukraine-invasion

3   Tony Bartleme, "The true and false stories of Anne Bonny, pirate woman of the Caribbean," (Charleston) *Post and Courier*, November 17, 2020.

4   Ibid.

5   Brian Hicks, "Blackbeard, Stede Bonnet and the end of piracy in Charles Town," (Charleston) *Post and Courier,* November 23, 2020.

6   Nicholas Butler, PhD, "The Charleston Pirate Trials of 1718," *Charleston Time Machine* podcast, Charleston County Public Library, November 30, 2018. Accessed at https://www.ccpl.org/charleston-time-machine/charleston-pirate -trials-1718, March 3, 2021.

7   See "The Chapels of Berkeley County."

8   Frank Richard Stockton, *Buccaneers and Pirates of Our Coast* (The Century Co., 1898). Within the public domain at https://www.gutenberg.org/files /17188/17188-h/17188-h.htm. Accessed March 3, 2021.

9   *Journal of the South Carolina Commons House of Assembly, 1716–21*, 154. Available on microfilm at South Carolina Department of Archives and History and at the Charleston County Public Library.
10 Butler, "The Charleston Pirate Trials of 1718."
11 Butler, "The Pirate Hunting Excursions of 1718."
12 Ian Watt, "Robinson Crusoe as a Myth," in *Essays in Criticism* (Norton Critical Edition, 1951; reprinted 1994).
13 Captain Charles Johnson(?), *A General History of the Robberies and Murders of the most notorious Pyrates* (London: Charles Rivington, J. Lacy, and J. Stone, 1724).

STEDE BONNET: CHARLES TOWN'S GENTLEMAN PIRATE

1   Lindley S. Butler, *Pirates, Privateers, & Rebel Raiders of the Carolina Coast* (Chapel Hill, NC: University of North Carolina Press, 2000), 275.
2   Amy Crawford, "The Gentleman Pirate," in *Smithsonian Magazine*, July 31, 2007.
3   Captain Charles Johnson (?), *A General History of the Robberies and Murders of the Most Notorious Pyrates* (London: Charles Rivington, J. Lacy, and J. Stone, 1724).
4   Crawford.
5   Faye Jensen, "December, 1718: The Pirate Stede Bonnet Is Hung in Charleston," in *This Month in SC's History*, blog of the South Carolina Historical Society, December 4, 2020.
6   Charleston's Pirates: An Informational Site on the Pirates of Charleston and Other Pirates of History (2003), http://www.charlestonpirates.com/stede_bonnet.html. Accessed May 4, 2021.
7   Hugh F. Rankin, "The Pirates of Colonial North Carolina, " North Carolina Department of Cultural Resources, 1960. Compiled and updated by Kathy Alexander, *Legends of America*; updated July 2020.
8   Charleston's Pirates: An Informational Site.
9   Robert Rosen, *A Short History of Charleston* (San Francisco: Lexikos, 1982. Updated and reprinted 1992), 15–17.
10 Rankin.
11 Dr. Nicholas Butler, "The Charleston Pirate Trials of 1718," episode 92 of *Charleston Time Machine* podcast, Charleston County Public Library,

November 30, 2018, https://www.ccpl.org/charleston-time-machine /charleston-pirate-trials-1718. Accessed May 6, 2021.

12 Ibid.

13 Public domain and available download as a PDF at http://lcweb2.loc.gov /service/lawlib/law0001/2010/201000158861859/201000158861859.pdf.

14 Rankin.

15 Ibid.

16 Ibid.

17 The North Carolina History Project, quoted by Hayley Fowler in "'Gentleman Pirate' was inept at sea, but it still got him hanged 301 years ago in SC," in the *Charlotte Observer*, December 10, 2019.

ANNE BONNY: THE REMARKABLE
ADVENTURES OF A FEMALE PYRATE

1 "By his Excellency; Woodes Rogers, Esq; Governour of New Providence, & c. A Proclamation," *Boston Gazette*, October 10–17, 1720.

2 Charles Johnson, *A General History of the Robberies and Murders of the Most Notorious Pyrates* (1724), East Carolina University Digital Collections at https://digital.lib.ecu.edu. Accessed May 8, 2021.

3 Karen Abbot, "If there's a man among ye: The Tale of Pirate Queens Anne Bonny and Mary Read," in *Smithsonian Magazine*, August 9, 2011.

4 "Anne Bonny," found in *The Way of the Pirates*, an Amazon Services LLC Associates Program, http://www.thewayofthepirates.com/famous-pirates /anne-bonny/. Accessed May 8, 2021.

5 Johnson.

6 Rob Canfield, "Something's Mizzen: Anne Bonny, Mary Read, 'Polly,' and Female Counter-Roles on the Imperialist Stage," in *South Atlantic Review*, vol. 66, No. 2, Spring 2001, 45–63.

7 "Ann Bonny and Mary Read convicted of Piracy Novr. 28th 1720" (1724), Rare Book Division, The New York Public Library, *The New York Public Library Digital Collections*, https://digitalcollections.nypl.org/items/8ae4f418 -cab6-888e-e040-e00a18064518. Accessed May 10, 2021.

8 "By his Excellency; Woodes Rogers, Esq; Governour of New Providence, & c. A Proclamation."

9 Johnson.

10 "Ann Bonny and Mary Read convicted of Piracy Novr. 28th 1720."

11   Tony Bartleme, "A 22-year-old YouTuber may have solved Anne Bonny pirate mystery 300 years after trial," in (Charleston) *Post and Courier*, January 19, 2021.

12   Ibid.

PART III: THE CODE DUELLO

1   Matthew H. Jennings, "Duelling," found in Walter Edgar (ed.), *South Carolina Encyclopedia* (Columbia, SC: The Humanities Council, 2006), 276.

2   Quote attributed to Dr. David Ramsey in Arthur H. Schaffer, *The Politics of History: Writing the History of the American Revolution, 1783–1815* (New Brunswick and London: Transaction Publishers, 2010), 72.

3   Jack K. Williams, *Dueling in the Old South* (College Station, TX, and London: Texas A & M University Press, 1980), 4.

4   John Lyde Wilson, *The Code of Honor, or Rules for the Government of Principals and Seconds in Duelling* (Charleston, SC: published by James Phinney in the rear of 18 Broad Street, 1838). In the public domain and available for download at https://books.google.com/books?id=usEiFvr XbF8C&printsec=frontcover&source=gbs_gesummary_r&cad=0#v=onepage &q&f=false. Accessed August 18, 2021.

5   Williams.

6   Wilson.

7   Jennings.

8   Ibid.

9   See "The Hopes and Horrors of Hampton Park."

10   Chris Egar, "The Firearms of the American Colonial Militia, Pre-1776," July 1, 2017 on the Guns.com website. Accessed August 18, 2021, at https:// www.guns.com/news/2017/07/01/guns-of-the-greatest-revolution-ever.

11   Jennings.

THE SAD DEMISE OF DR. JOSEPH BROWN LADD

1   Wesley Pippenger, *Tombstone Inscriptions of Alexandria, Virginia*, vol. 1 (1992); inscription originally transcribed from Timothy Alden's *A Collection of American Epitaphs and Inscriptions*, 1814. Viewable at Findagrave.com, Memorial to Joseph Brown Ladd as inscribed on the box tomb of his mother, Sarah Gardner Ladd, in the Old Presbyterian Meeting House churchyard,

Alexandria, VA. Accessed August 18, 2021, at https://www.findagrave.com /memorial/104202614/joseph-brown-ladd.

2   Joseph Brown Ladd, MD, *The literary remains of Joseph Brown Ladd, M.D.— A sketch of the Author's Life*, collected by his sister, Mrs. Elizabeth Ladd Haskins, of Rhode Island. To which is prefixed: *A sketch of the author's life*, by W. B. Chittenden. (New York: H. C. Sleight, 1832), v.

3   Ibid., xviii.

4   Ibid., xiii.

5   Ibid., xix.

6   *Charleston Morning News and Daily Advertiser*, October 12, 1786. Accessed at https://www.newspapers.com/newspage/78155174/, August 18, 2021.

7   Ladd.

PART IV: THE FAMOUS, INFAMOUS, AND MOSTLY FORGOTTEN

1   Peter N. Starnes, "Why Study History?" American Historical Association, found at https://www.historians.org/about-aha-and-membership/aha-history -and-archives/historical-archives/why-study-history-(1998). Accessed August 22, 2021.

2   Someone once said, and I can't remember who, that our history has been made, if not written, by average, everyday people just trying to make enough money to pay the rent and keep their families fed.

3   Headstone of Elizabeth (Eliza) Lucas Pinckney (1723–1793), St. Peter's Episcopal Churchyard, Philadelphia, Pennsylvania. Available at https://www .findagrave.com/memorial/28036633/elizabeth-pinckney. Accessed August 22, 2021.

4   John McDermott, "On business: High-income earners make inroads in South Carolina," in *Charleston Post and Courier*, September 14, 2020.

5   Some accounts suggest that her brother may have traveled with her at least part of the way.

6   Leigh Jones Handal, "John and Affra (nee Harleston) Coming," at Charleston Raconteurs.com, http://www.charlestonraconteurs.com/coming-john-and -affra.html. Accessed on August 22, 2021.

7   Additional individuals' stories can be found in "The Chapels of Berkeley County."

MARY FISHER BAYLEY CROSS: A WOMAN ON A MISSION

1 Stefano Villani, "Fisher (married names Bayly, Cross), Mary (c. 1623–1698), Quaker missionary," in *Oxford Dictionary of National Biography*, n.p.

2 Joseph Besse, 1683?–1757, *Sufferings of Early Quakers* (York, England: Sessions Book Trust, 1998), 84–85.

3 E. Digby Baltzell, *Puritan Boston & Quaker Philadelphia* (Piscataway, NJ: Transaction Publishers, 1979), 86.

4 Ibid.

5 Janet Moore Lindman and Michele Lise Tarter (eds.), *A Centre of Wonders: The Body in Early America* (Ithaca, NY, and London: Cornell University Press, 2001), x, 284.

6 "Ann Austin and Mary Fisher Arrested," Christianity.com, Salem Web Network.

7 *Quaker Faith and Practice: The Book of Christian Discipline of the Yearly Meeting of the Religious Society of Friends (Quakers) in Britain* (Quaker Books, 2005), n.p.

8 Besse, 388.

9 James Bowden, *The History of the Society of Friends in America*, vol. 1 (United States: BiblioBazaar, 2016). Abstract of a letter from Robert Barrow to his wife dated 12 Mo. 1696/7, n.p.

10 A. S. Salley, "Abstracts from the Records of the Court of Ordinary of the Province of South Carolina, 1700–1712 (Continued)," in *The South Carolina Historical and Genealogical Magazine*, vol. 12, no. 2, 1911, 70–71.

11 Ibid.

AMERICA'S FIRST CREMATION

1 Will of Henry Laurens, dated 1 November 1792, proved on 7 January 1793. Charleston County Will Book B (1786–1793), 712; transcribed in WPA transcript volume 24C (1786–1793), 1152–58.

CARADEUX THE CRUEL

1 Geni.com, Jean Baptiste "The Cruel" Caradeuc public profile, at https://www.geni.com/people/Jean-Caradeuc/6000000094916255847. Accessed August 19, 2021.

2   David Geggus (ed.), "The Caradeaux and Colonial Memory," in *The Impact of the Haitian Revolution in the Atlantic World* (Columbia, SC: University of South Carolina Press, 2001).

3   David Geggus, "The British Government and the Saint-Domingue Slave Revolt, 1791–1793," in *The English Historical Review* (New York: Oxford University Press, April 1982), 1.

4   Emmanuel Moise Yves, "The Caradeux Zone," on ayiboPOST, at https://ayibopost.com/la-zone-caradeux-porte-le-nom-de-lesclavagiste-le-plus-criminel-de-lhistoire-dhaiti/. Accessed August 19, 2021.

5   Cyril Lionel Robert James, *The Black Jacobins: Toussaint L'Ouverture and the San Domingo Revolution* (Open Library Internet Archive: Secker & Warburg Ltd., 1938).

6   Geggus, "The Caradeaux and Colonial Memory."

7   Mabel L. Webber, "Copy of Some Loose Pages found among the Manigault Papers, in the Handwriting of Dr. Gabriel Manigault, October 25, 1888," in *South Carolina Historical and Genealogical Magazine*, 15.

8   Margaret Wilson Gillikin, *Saint Dominguan Refugees in Charleston, South Carolina, 1791–1822: Assimilation and Accommodation in a Slave Society*, doctoral dissertation (University of South Carolina, 2014). Accessed at https://scholarcommons.sc.edu/etd/3040, August 19, 2021.

JOHN AND LAVINIA FISHER:
THE TRUTH BEHIND THE LEGEND

1   A definitive answer as to who was the first woman to be executed for murder in the United States is elusive. Mary Surratt is generally believed to be the first woman hanged for murder by the federal government (on July 7, 1865, for the assassination of President Abraham Lincoln). However, based on various caveats, a number of other women share some version of this claim. In "Lessons from History" (January 11, 2020), Dale L. Brumfield cites the hanging of Jane Champion c. 1632 in Jamestown, Virginia, as the first female execution for infanticide, immediately following the birth of her illegitimate child. Murderpedia lists a former passenger on the *Mayflower*, Alicia Martin Bishop, as the first woman hanged in the colonies for killing her four-year-old daughter in 1648 in Plymouth, Massachusetts. Bathsheba Ruggles Spooner was the first woman executed in the newly declared United States of America on July 2, 1778, for conspiracy to commit the murder of her husband. In

1902, Jane Toppan (b. Honora Kelley) confessed to thirty-one murders, but was declared insane and sentenced to live her natural life within the confines of an insane asylum. Surprisingly, it seems that perhaps Aileen Wuornos truly may have been the first female serial killer executed for murder, a sentence that was carried out in Florida on October 9, 2002.

2 For more about the trading route to the site of George Chicken's camp and the St. James Chapel of Ease, see "The Chapels of Berkeley County."

3 *Charleston Courier*, February 20, 1819.

4 Ibid.

5 *Charleston Courier*, February 22, 1819.

6 For more about the Charleston District Jail, see "The Horrors of the Old Public Square."

7 *Charleston Courier*, February 19, 1820.

8 For more about Potter's Field, see "The Horrors of the Old Public Square."

DEATH OF THE CAROLINA PARAKEET

1 "The Last Carolina Parakeet," John Jay Audubon Center at Mill Grove, https://johnjames.audubon.org/last-carolina-parakeet. Accessed May 26, 2021.

2 John Jay Audubon, *Birds of America; from original drawings* (London: published by the author in a series, 1827–1838), plate 26. Accessed at https://www.audubon.org/birds-of-america/carolina-parrot#, May 25, 2021.

3 Ibid.

4 "Carolina Parakeet," *Wikipedia*. Accessed May 25, 2021.

5 Emily Jack, "Meet Doodles, the Carolina Parakeet," in *Tarhellia*, blog of the University of North Carolina Library, July 11, 2012. Accessed May 25, 2021.

6 Dieter Luther, *Die ausgestorbenen Vogel dre Welt [The extinct birds of the world]*, 4th edition (Heidelberg, Germany: Westarp-Wissenschaften).

PART V: PLACES WITH A PAST

THE CHAPELS OF BERKELEY COUNTY: STORIES OF WORSHIP, WAR, BETRAYAL, AND FEAR

1 Much of the information in this essay has been gathered through the author's research on behalf of the St. James Goose Creek Chapel of Ease/Bethlehem Baptist Historic Site (www.chapelofease.org). The author gratefully acknowledges the research (and friendship) of Michael Heitzler, EdD, author

of *Goose Creek: A Definitive History,* vol. I & II (Charleston, SC: The History Press, 2005 and 2006); *The Goose Creek Bridge: Gateway to Sacred Places* (Bloomington, IN: AuthorHouse LLC, 2012); and *The Chicken Trilogy* (Bloomington, IN: AuthorHouse LLC, 2017).

2   Walter B. Edgar (ed.), Inez Watson, research consultant, *Biographical Directory of the South Carolina House of Representatives, Volume 1, 1692–1973* (Columbia, SC: University of South Carolina Press), 153.

3   Alan Gallay, *The Indian Slave Trade: The Rise of the English Empire in the American South,* 1670–1717 (New York: Yale University Press), 299.

4   Verner W. Crane, *The Southern Frontier, 1670–1732* (Ann Arbor, MI: University of Michigan Press, 1956), 168–69.

5   The Reverend Francis LeJau, *The Carolina Chronicle of Dr. Francis Le Jau* (Berkeley, CA: University of California, 1956).

6   Michael Heitzler, EdD, *The Goose Creek Bridge: Gateway to Sacred Places* (Bloomington, IN: Author House LLC Publishing 2012), 58–59.

7   Ibid, 64.

8   Heitzler, *The Goose Creek Bridge,* 61.

9   Richard Traunter, *Travels of Richard Traunter of the Main Continent of America from Appomattox River in Virginia to Charles Town in South Carolina, Two Journals 1698, 1699* (Richmond, VA: Virginia Historical Society), 4–5.

10   Ibid.

11   Frank J. Klingberg, *The Carolina Chronicle of Reverend Francis LeJau,* 1707–1717 (Los Angeles: University of California Press, 1956), 152.

12   Heitzler, *The Goose Creek Bridge,* 66.

13   Walter J. Fraser, *Lowcountry Hurricanes* (Athens, GA: The University of Georgia Press, 2006), 11.

14   Cecil Headlam (ed.), *Calendar of State Papers, Colonial Series, American and the West Indies,* 1716–1717 (London, 1922)

15   Heitzler, *The Goose Creek Bridge,* 65–66.

16   Frank J. Klingberg, *The Carolina Chronicle of Reverend Francis LeJau, 1707–1717* (Los Angeles: University of California Press, 1956), 158–159.

17   Michael Heitzler, EdD, *The Goose Creek Bridge: Gateway to Sacred Places* (Bloomington, IN: AuthorHouse LLC Publishing, 2012), 78.

18   John K. Mahon and Brent R. Weisman, "Florida's Seminole and Miccosukee Peoples," in Michael Gannon (ed.), *The New History of Florida* (Gainesville, FL: University Press of Florida, 1996), 183. As a side note, the Seminoles would again challenge the Charles Town settlers' descendants more than a

century later in 1835 under the leadership of their renowned chief, Osceola, who was held prisoner at Fort Moultrie on Sullivan's Island for three months before he died January 30, 1838, probably of complications from tonsillitis. A man respected even by his adversaries, Osceola was buried at the fort with military honors. His grave remains there and is visited by thousands each year who come to pay their respects.

19 Steven J. Oatis, *A Colonial Complex: South Carolina's Frontiers in the Era of the Yamasee War, 1680–1730* (Lincoln, NE: University of Nebraska Press, 2004), 167.

20 Michael J. Heitzler, EdD, and Jennie Haskell Rose, *The Chicken Trilogy* (Bloomington, IN: AuthorHouse, 2017), 91.

21 Michael J. Heitzler, EdD, *Goose Creek: A Definitive History*, vol. 1 (Charleston, SC: The History Press, 2005), 265.

22 FindaGrave.com/memorial/31481035/archibald-broun. Accessed August 8, 2021.

23 J. Russell Cross, *Historic Ramblings Through Berkeley* (Columbia, SC: Cross-Williams Family Limited Partnership, 1985), 206–207.

24 Heitzler, *Goose Creek*, vol 1., 116.

25 Michael J. Heitzler, EdD, *Goose Creek: A Definitive History*, vol. 2 (Charleston, SC: The History Press 2006), 26.

26 Some of the information in this essay is drawn from Leigh Jones Handal, *Lost Charleston* (London: Pavilion Publishing, 2019), 9.

27 Mrs. Arthur Gordon Rose, *Little Mistress Chicken: A Veritable Happening of Colonial Carolina* (Columbia, SC: R. L. Bryan Company, 1969), 10

28 Mrs. Arthur Gordon Rose, *Little Mistress Chicken: A Veritable Happening of Colonial Carolina* (Columbia, SC: R. L. Bryan Company, 1969).

29 Ibid., 8.

30 Ibid., Preface by Robert S. Solomon, MD, and Gary C. LeCroy.

31 Ibid., 14.

32 Ibid., 20.

33 Martha Sullivan, in an interview with Debi Chard, *WSCS Live5 News*, "Woman remembers 70-year-old discovery of buried Berkeley Co. treasure," July 18, 2017.

34 Grahame Long, in an interview with Debi Chard, *WSCS Live5 News*, "Woman remembers 70-year-old discovery of buried Berkeley Co. treasure," July 18, 2017.

35   "French Huguenots Flee to South Carolina," in *Summerville Scene*, October 14, 2020.

36   Robert Shelton Converse, "St. Thomas and St. Denis Parish Church: An AngloFranco Alliance in the Lowcountry," doctoral dissertation presented to The Graduate Schools of Clemson University and the College of Charleston, May 2011.

37   Ibid.

38   Melinda Meeks Hennessy, "Racial Violence During Reconstruction: The 1876 Riots in Charleston and Cainhoy," in *South Carolina Historical Magazine*, vol. 86, no. 2, April 1985, 104–06.

THE HOPES AND HORRORS OF HAMPTON PARK

1   For more on the life and legacy of Denmark Vesey, see David M. Robertson, *Denmark Vesey: The Buried Story of America's Largest Slave Rebellion and the Man Who Led It* (Knopf, 1999). For more on the life and legacy of Wade Hampton, see Rod Andrew Jr., *Wade Hampton: Confederate Warrior to Southern Redeemer* (Chapel Hill, NC: University of North Carolina Press, 2008). There are many other sources available as well.

2   SCIWAY, South Carolina's Informational Highway website, https://www.sciway.net/hist/indians/geo.html.

3   "A Historic Architectural Resources Survey of the Upper Peninsula Charleston, South Carolina," an unpublished report prepared by John Beaty, Architectural Historian, and Ralph Bailey, Principal Investigator, on behalf of Brockington and Associates, Inc., for the City of Charleston Design, Development and Preservation Department, January 2004.

4   Kevin Eberle, *A History of Hampton Park* (Charleston, SC: The History Press, 2012), 17–19.

5   Ibid.

6   Alexander Garden, *Anecdotes of the American Revolution: Illustrative of the Talents and Virtues of the Heroes and Patriots, who Acted the Most Conspicuous Parts Therein*, vol. 1–3 (Charleston, SC: A. E. Miller, 1828).

7   Eberle, 26.

8   *Johann Ewald's Memoirs: A Hessian captain's notes on the Revolutionary War*, written in 1881. Translated by Joseph P. Tustin (New Haven, CT: Yale University Press, 1979).

9   Eberle, 28.

10 Ibid.

11 John Beaufain Irving, *The South Carolina Jockey Club, Charleston 1857*, South Carolina Jockey Club Records, manuscript collection of the Charleston Library Society.

12 Eberle, 33.

13 Peter Benes, "Table 1.4 Twenty-Four Year American Itinerary of English-Born William Frederick Pincbeck: For a Short Time Only" (University of Massachusetts Press: Supplemental Material). Retrieved from https://scholarworks.umass.edu/umpress_short_time_only/13

14 "The Martyrs of the Race Course," *Charleston Daily Courier*, May 2, 1865.

15 Dr. David W. Blight, "The First Decoration Day," in the *Newark Star Ledger*, April 27, 2015.

16 Eberle, 106.

17 Ibid., 107.

THE TAIL OF WASHINGTON'S HORSE

1 Anna Wells Rutledge, *Catalogue of Paintings and Sculpture in the Council Chamber, City Hall, Charleston, South Carolina* (Charleston, SC: The City Council, 1943).

2 Dr. Nicholas Butler, *Charleston Time Machine* podcast, episode 90, November 9, 2018. Charleston County Public Library, https://www.ccpl.org/charleston-time-machine/tail-washingtons-horse. Accessed August 21, 2021.

3 Ibid.

4 Ibid.

5 John Trumbull, *Autobiography, Reminiscences and Letters of John Trumbull from 1756 to 1841* (New York: Wiley and Putnam, 1841).

6 Rutledge.

7 Butler.

8 T. H. Breen, *George Washington's Journey: The President Forges a New Nation* (New York: Simon & Schuster, 2016).

CHARLESTON'S PUBLIC SQUARE:
HELL, WICKED PLACES, AND GREAT JAZZ

1 Dr. Nicholas Butler, "The Forgotten Dead: Charleston's Public Cemeteries, 1672–1794," *Charleston Time Machine* podcast, Charleston County Public

Library, April 30, 2021. Accessed at https://www.ccpl.org/charleston-time
-machine/forgotten-dead-charlestons-public-cemeteries-1672-1794#_edn8
on August 23, 2021.

2   *Journal of His Majesty's Council for South Carolina*, no. 10, November 9,
1743, 391–92, found in the collections of the South Carolina Department of
Archives and History, Columbia, South Carolina.

3   Christine Trebellas, *Charleston County Jail* (Washington, DC: Historic
American Buildings Survey, 1995), 24. Quoted in David C. Scott, *Abode
of Misery: An Illustrated Compilation of Facts, Secrets and Myths of the Old
Charleston District Jail* (Charleston, SC: Building Arts Press, 2010), 33.

4   Ibid.

5   Ibid.

6   "225 Years of History," the Medical Society of South Carolina website.
Accessed at https://www.medsocietysc.com/history/ on August 23, 2021.

7   Jonathan H. Poston for Historic Charleston Foundation, *The Buildings of
Charleston: A Guide to the City's Architecture* (Columbia, SC: University of
South Carolina Press, 1997), 392.

8   "Through the Years, A History of Roper Hospital," on the Roper St. Francis
Healthcare website. Accessed at https://www.rsfh.com/about/history/ on
August 23, 2021.

9   Captain Luis F. Emilio, *A Brave Black Regiment, The History of the 54th
Massachusetts, 1863–1865* (Boston: The Boston Book Company, 2nd edition,
1894), 401. Quoted in David C. Scott, *Abode of Misery: An Illustrated
Compilation of Facts, Secrets and Myths of the Old Charleston District Jail*
(Charleston, SC: Building Arts Press, 2010), 114.

10 Joseph Williams, "Charleston's Work House and Sugar House," in *College of
Charleston Discovering Our Past* blog. Accessed at https://discovering.cofc.edu
/items/show/31?tour=4&index=5 on August 24, 2021.

11 James Matthews, as told to Joshua Levitte in The Emancipator, September
20, 1838. Accessed at https://docsouth.unc.edu/neh/runaway/runaway.html
on August 24, 2021.

12 Ibid.

13 Williams.

14 *Charleston News and Courier*, September 2, 1886.

15 Some writers claim as many as forty thousand people have died at the
Old District Jail. However, David C. Scott, author of *Abode of Misery: An
Illustrated Compilation of Facts, Secrets and Myths of the Old Charleston District*

Jail (Charleston, SC: Building Arts Press, 2010), disputes that that many deaths could be attributable to the District Jail, as doing so would suggest more than three hundred deaths a year, or nearly one a day over its 136 years of operation, a number not supported by contemporary news accounts. Most historians set the number closer to ten thousand.

16   Even *Wikipedia* incorrectly lists it by this name.

17   David B. Scott, *Abode of Misery: An Illustrated Compilation of the Facts, Secrets and Myths of the Old Charleston District Jail* (Charleston, SC: Building Arts Press, 2010), 4.

18   Robert Mills is perhaps better known nationally as the architect of the Washington Monument and US Treasury Building in the nation's capital, as well as First Baptist Church and the Fireproof Building, among others, in Charleston.

19   The window to the east of the author's office during her tenure working there with the American College of the Building Arts can be seen in this image—second floor, far right. In November 2019, she accepted a dare to spend a night in one of the old jail cells with a couple of fellow history buffs. Though a proclaimed skeptic of the paranormal, she has now checked that item off her bucket list and won't do it again.

20   Jonathan H. Poston for Historic Charleston Foundation, *The Buildings of Charleston: A Guide to the City's Architecture* (Columbia, SC: University of South Carolina Press, 1997), 392.

21   The veracity and details of the Slave Uprising of 1822 continue to be debated today, though a thorough discussion of the topic is outside the scope of this retelling of the accused's incarceration in the District Jail.

22   Douglas R. Edgerton, "Vesey, Denmark," in the *South Carolina Encyclopedia*, Walter Edgar (ed.) (Columbia, SC: The Humanities Council, 2006), 999.

23   James W. Hagy, *City Directories for Charleston, South Carolina for the Years 1803, 1806, 1807, 1809 and 1813* (Baltimore, MD: Genealogical Publishing Co., 2000).

24   "Jacque Alexander Tardy," *Wikipedia*. Accessed https://en.wikipedia.org/wiki/Jacque_Alexander_Tardy#cite_note-2 on August 29, 2021.

25   Roger Pickenpaugh, *Captives in Blue: The Civil War Prisons of the Confederacy* (Tuscaloosa, AL: University of Alabama Press), 12.

26   "Charleston County Jail Prisoner of War Camp," in *The American Civil War*. Accessed at https://www.mycivilwar.com/pow/sc-charleston-county-jail.html on August 29, 2021.

27 "A Century of Lawmaking for a New Nation: US Congressional Documents and Debates, 1774–1875," published in the *Statutes at Large* of the Fifth Congress, Second Session, of the United States, 605. Within the public domain and accessible through the Library of Congress at http://memory.loc .gov/cgi-bin/ampage?collId=llsl&fileName=001/llsl001.db&recNum=728.

28 Jonathan Poston for Historic Charleston Foundation, *The Buildings of Charleston: A Guide to the City's Architecture* (Columbia, SC: The University of South Carolina Press, 1997), 352.

29 "Old Marine Hospital," in the *South Carolina Picture Project*. Accessed at https://www.scpictureproject.org/charleston-county/old-marine-hospital.html on August 30, 2021.

30 Some of the research for this piece is taken from Leigh Jones Handal, *Lost Charleston* (London: Pavilion Publishing, 2019), 92–95.

31 Or at least he was one of the first to introduce the steps, depending on one's source.

32 Some sources say the dance was introduced even earlier in an off-Broadway musical titled *Liza*, though certainly it was *Running Wild* that brought the dance to national prominence.

PART VI: THE CURSE OF THE BRACKISH WATER

THE DRIEST PLACE ON EARTH

1 Walter J. Fraser Jr., *Charleston! Charleston!* (Columbia, SC: University of South Carolina Press, 1989), 4.

2 Ibid., 22.

3 Ibid., 5.

4 Ibid., 22.

5 Ibid., 11.

6 Robert Rosen, *A Short History of Charleston* (San Francisco: Lexikos, 1982. Updated and reprinted 1992), 33.

7 Thomas Cooper (ed.), *The Statutes at Large of South Carolina*, vol. II (Columbia, SC, 1837), 1–6.

8 Joseph I. Waring, *The First Voyage and Settlement at Charles Town*, 1670–1680. Published for the South Carolina Tricentennial Commission by the South Carolina Press: 1st edition (January 1, 1970), 25–31.

9 Paul R. Hibbard, "A History of South Carolina Liquor Regulation," in *South Carolina Law Review*, vol. 19, issue 2, Article 1, 1967, 167.

THE RISE OF PITCHFORK BEN TILLMAN

1 Lacy K. Ford Jr., "Origins of the Edgefield Tradition: The Late Antebellum Experience and the Roots of Political Insurgency," in *The South Carolina Historical Magazine*, October 1997, 328–48.

2 Stephen Kantrowitz, *Ben Tillman and the Reconstruction of White Supremacy* (Chapel Hill, NC: University of North Carolina Press, 2000), 22–24.

3 "'Pitchfork' Ben Tillman: The Most Lionized Figure in South Carolina History," in *The Journal of Blacks in Higher Education*, Winter 2007–2008, 48–49.

4 Key among Tillman's legacy is adoption of the South Carolina State Constitution of 1895, which disenfranchised most of the state's black majority, as well as many poor whites, and ensured that the white Democratic Party would remain in power until the election of Republican governor James B. Edwards in 1975.

5 "HISTORY: Pitchfork Ben Tillman, Governor, US Senator," in *Charleston Currents*, November 14, 2016.

6 Brian Hicks, "Grand exposition features bout between Charleston, Tillman," in (Charleston) *Post and Courier*, December 6, 2020.

7 Stephen Kantrowitz, "Ben Tillman and Hendrix McLane, Agrarian Rebels: White Manhood, 'The Farmers,' and the Limits of Southern Populism," in *The Journal of Southern History*, August 2000, 497–524.

8 "'Pitchfork' Ben Tillman," 48–49.

THE DISPENSARY ACT OF 1893

1 As had King Charles II's, so many years before, as noted in chapter 1.

2 Kevin Michael Krause, *A Different State of Mind: Ben Tillman and the Transformation of State Government in South Carolina, 1885–1895*, doctoral dissertation submitted to the Graduate Faculty of the University of Georgia, Athens, Georgia, 2014.

3 Francis Butler Simkins, *Pitchfork Ben Tillman, South Carolinian* (Baton Rouge, LA: Louisiana State University Press, 1944), 257–259.

4 "Those Pre-Pro Whiskey Men" blog. Accessed at http://pre-prowhiskeymen .blogspot.com/2020/07/how-vincent-chicco-bested-notorious.html on May 20, 2021.

VINCENT CHICCO: KING OF THE BLIND TIGERS

1 Stephen Kantrowitz, *Ben Tillman and the Reconstruction of White Supremacy* (Chapel Hill, NC: University of North Carolina Press, 2000), 189.
2 "Those Pre-Pro Whiskey Men" blog. Accessed at http://pre-prowhiskeymen .blogspot.com/2020/07/how-vincent-chicco-bested-notorious.html, May 20, 2021.
3 *State ex rel. Lyon, Atty. Gen. vs. Chicco*, Supreme Court of South Carolina, January 11, 1909.
4 "Those Pre-Pro Whiskey Men."
5 Ibid.

INDEX

116–17; Church of St. Thomas and St. Denis of, 132–36, *133*; Goose Creek Men and, 12; LeJau in, 109; Quakers and, 79; St. Philip's, 163, 195

Animal Welfare Act of 1971, 155

Anne (Queen), 19

aristocracy, 7; Tillman, B., and, 199; at Washington Race Course, 147

Articles of Confederation, 85

arts, in Charleston, 18–19

Asylum for the Deaf and Dumb, 165

Audubon, John J., *100*, 101

Austin, Ann, 79–80

Baker, Josephine, *189*

Ball, Elias, II, 127

Ball, Keating Simons, 130–31, *131*

Ball, William Watts, 199

Barbados: Bonnet from, 39, 41; Moore, J., I, from, 110; Quakers in, 79–80; sugar plantations in, 11, 39, 79

Barbot, Louis J., 173

Barker, Thomas, 109, 112–13; Moore, J., I, and, 110

Barnet, Jonathan, 57

Barrow, Richard, 83

Bartsch, Paul, 101, *101*

Bayley, Mary, 82; inheritance of, 83–84

Bayley, Susannah, 82; inheritance of, 83–84

Bayley, William, Jr., 82; inheritance of, 83

Bayley, William, Sr., 82

Beauclerk, Charles, 28

Beauclerk, James, 28

Bedchamber Crisis, 26

Bellamy, Catherine, 106

Bellingham, Richard, 79–80

Belmont, August, Jr., 154

Belmont Park, horse racing at, 154

Bethlehem Baptist Church, *107*, 117–22

Biggins Church, 124

bilious fever, 122

Birds of America (Audubon), *100*

Bishop, Alicia Martin, 219n1

Blackbeard. *See* Teach, Edward

Blind Tiger exhibition halls, 203–4; of Chicco, 205–8, *206*

Bonnet, Stede, 36, 39–52, *42*; from Barbados, 39, 41; at District Jail, 172; escape attempt of, 50–51; hanging of, 52, 215n17; Johnson, Robert, and, 44–45, 50; plantations of, 39–40; pleas for mercy by, 51–52; Rhett and, 44–48, 51, 52; Teach and, 43–44, 51; trial of, 48–50, *49*

Bonny, Anne, 53–59, *54*; as illegitimate child, 54–55; in Nassau, 55–56; pregnancy of, 57, 58–59; Rackham and, 56–57, 58; trial of, 57–58; unknown end of, 59

Bonny, James, 55–56

Braithwaite, John, 139

A Brave Black Regiment (Emilio), 165–67

Breen, T. H., 161

Brennan, Mary "Peg," 55

Brewton, Miles, 14, *14*; Strawberry Chapel and, 132
Bright, David, 147
Broun, Archibald, 121–22
Broun, Elizabeth Thomas, 120
Broun, Robert, 120
Brown, Morris, 177
Brown, Russell, 187–88
Brumfield, Dale L., 219n1
Bryan, William Jennings, *201*
Butler, Nicholas, 47–48, 53, 156–57, 161

Cainhoy Massacre, 132–36
Calico Jack (Rackham, John), 56–57, 58
Calvinists, 3; plantations of, 10–11. *See also* Huguenots
Cantey, John, 145
Caradeux, Jean-Baptiste: to Charleston, 90–91; in Saint-Domingue, 88–90; sexual abuse by, 89
Carey-Cothran Law, 207
Carolina parakeet, extinction of, *100*, 100–102, *101*
carpetbaggers, 134
Cartwright, Daniel, 139
Cassique, 138
Castle Pinckney, 180, *181*
Catherine of Braganza, 16, 21–23, *22*; Palmer, B., and, 25–26; Pennancoët and, 29–30
Catholics: after American Revolution, 11; in Charleston, 10, 11; Hibernian Society and, 11;

Louis XIV as, 9; ostracized in Charleston, 10; Palmer, B., as, 27
Chamberlain, Daniel Henry, 136
Champion, Jane, 219n1
chapels: of Charleston, 104–36. *See also* St. James Goose Creek Chapel of Ease; Strawberry Chapel
Chard, Debi, 132
Charles I, 2–3; Coming and, 76
Charles II, *ix*, *2*, *3*, *7*; arts and, 18–19; Catherine of Braganca and, 16, 21–23, *22*; as Charleston namesake, 2–8; in Church of England, 9; cockfighting and, 17; Divine Rights of, 6; Gwyn and, *27*, 27–29; Hampton Park and, 139; horse racing and, 16; illegitimate children of, 4, 21, 23, 24–25, 28, 30, 31; Kéroualle and, 29–31, *30*; Palmer, B., and, 23–27, *26*; Walter and, 4, *5*, 21
Charleston (city), ix–x; alcohol in, 194–96, 202–8; arts in, 18–19; Caradeux to, 90–91; Carolina parakeet in, *100*, 100–102, *101*; Catholics in, 10, 11; chapels of, 104–36; Charles II as namesake of, 2–8; City Hall of, 156–61, *157*, *159*, *161*; cockfighting in, 17; cremations in, 85–87; dueling in, 62–72; as The Holy City, 9–12; horse racing in, 16; Old Public Square in, 162–91, *166*; pirates of, 34–59; in Reconstruction, 147; religious

illegitimate children: Bonny, A., as, 54–55; of Charles II, 4, 21, 23, 24–25, 28, 30, 31

Indian Hill, 139

indigo, 13, 34, 120

Isaacs, Ralph, III, 70–72, *72*

Ivory City: Cotton Palace at, 150, *150*, *151*; Eskimo Village at, 150, *152*; in Hampton Park, 148, 149–50, *150*; horse racing at, *152*

Jacobites, 40, 44

jail. *See* District Jail

James, C. L. R., 89

James, Lena, 184

James II and VII, 4, 9; Gwyn and, 28, 29; Penancoët and, 31

James Island, 141

Jane (Lady), *3*

jazz: Charleston dance and, 188–89, *189*, *190*; Jenkins Orphanage Band and, 167, 187–88, *188*, *190*, 190–91

Jenkins, Daniel, 184–90, *186*; death of, 190

Jenkins Orphanage, 185–87

Jenkins Orphanage Band, 167, 187–88, *188*, *190*, 190–91

Jensen, C. A., *141*

Jews, 11

Johnson, Charles, 38, 40, 41, *42*, 53, *54*, 56, 57, 59

Johnson, James P., 188

Johnson, Ralph H., 76–77, *77*

Johnson, Robert, 37; Bonnet and, 44–45, 50; pirates' hanging and, 51; Teach and, 43

Katherine of Aragon, 22

Kéroualle, Louise Renée de Penancoët de, 29–31, *30*

Killigrew, Elizabeth, 31

King's Pardon, for pirates, 44

Kline, Krystle, 20–21

Ladd, Joseph Ladd, 68–72, *69*, *72*, 216n1; poems of, 68, 70, 71–72

Ladd, Sarah, 68

Ladd, William, 68

Lafayette, Marquis de, 121

Laurens, Henry, 85–87, *86*

Laurens, John, 86

Learned Pig, 144

Leavitt, Joshua, 168–69

Lee, Henry "Light Horse Harry," III, 139

LeJau, Francis, 12, 109, 113, 115

Lely, James, *30*

Levit, John, 50

The literary remains of Joseph Brown Ladd, M.D. (Haskins), 72

Liza (off-Broadway musical), 227n32

Locke, John, 10, 11; cockfighting and, 17

Long, Grahame, 132

long rooms, 195

Loocock, Aaron, 120–21

Loocock, Mary Broun, 120

Lords Proprietors, 5, 6; on alcohol, 195; marketing by, 13; pirates and, 36; Queen Anne and, 19; religious tolerance of, 9–10; Yamasee War and, 37

Louis XIII, 3

Louis XIV, 3, 29; Catholicism of,

Simmons, William E., 135
Simons, Benjamin, III, 128
Simons, Catherine Chicken, 126–31
Six-Mile House, 92–94
Slave Rebellion of 1791, in Saint-
    Domingue, 89–90, 178
Slave Rebellion of 1822, 177–78,
    226n21
slaves and slavery: Caradeux and,
    88–91; at District Jail, 173,
    177–78; at Hampton Park,
    137–38, 144; hanging of,
    89; Jenkins as, 184; Native
    Americans as, 107, 110; Quakers
    and, 11, 84; at Sugar House,
    167–71, *169*, *170. See also*
    plantations
smallpox, 165
Smith, William Loughton,
    158–61, *161*
Society for the Propagation of
    the Gospel in Foreign Parts
    (SPGFP), 12, 109, 113
Society of Friends. *See* Quakers
Some Observations and Directions
    for the Culture of Madder
    (Loocock, A.), 120
South, Stanley A., 139
South-Carolina Gazette: theater
    advertisement in, 19; Timothy,
    P., at, 120–21
South Carolina Inter-State and West
    Indian Exposition of 1901–1902.
    See Ivory City
South Carolina Jockey Club, 16,
    143–44, 147–48; Washington,
    G., and, 158

South Carolina State Constitution,
    228n4
Spencer, Diana, 31
Spenlow, Thomas, 58
SPGFP. *See* Society for the
    Propagation of the Gospel in
    Foreign Parts
Spoleto Festival, 19
Spooner, Bathsheba Ruggles, 219n1
The State That Forgot (Ball, W.), 199
Statistics of South Carolina (Mills),
    164–65, 173–74
Stearns, Peter N., 74
Stevens, Robert, 111
St. James Goose Creek Chapel of
    Ease, 105, *107*, 116–22; Broun,
    A., at, 121–22; Broun, E., at,
    120; Broun, R., at, 120; Loocock,
    A., at, 120–21; Shier at, 122
St. John's Berkeley Parish
    Church, 124
Stolen Charleston (Long), 132
St. Philip's Anglican Church,
    163, 195
Strawberry Chapel, 105, 124–25,
    125; Chicken, C., at, 126–31;
    silver at, 130–32, *131*
Strawberry Ferry, *123*, 125; Chicken,
    L., and, 126
Stuart, James, 40
Sugar House, 167–71, *169*, *170*;
    District Jail and, 177; in Great
    Earthquake of 1886, 182
sugar plantations: in Barbados, 11,
    39, 79; Native American slaves
    on, 107. *See also* Slave Rebellion
    of 1791

West, J. H., 148
Whitney, Eli, 13
William (Prince), 31
William II, Prince of Orange, 4
Williamson, Atkin, 195
Wilmot, John, 8, 210n8
Wilson, James, 50
Wilson, John Lyde, 62–64, *63*
Wooten, Elizabeth, 79
Wragg, Samuel, 43

Wright, John Michael, *7*
Wuornos, Aileen, 219n1

Yamasee War, 37, 108–10, 112–13;
    Chicken, G., in, 109, 113–16;
    Mulberry Castle in, 114, *114*
yellow fever epidemic, 116, 122, 165
Young, Seth, 96

zoo, at Hampton Park, 137, 154–55

ABOUT THE AUTHOR

A native South Carolinian, Leigh Jones Handal has been an avid student of Charleston's history since she first stepped foot in the Holy City on a Brownie Scout field trip. A graduate of the College of Charleston with an MA degree in journalism from the University of South Carolina, Handal has been a licensed city tour guide for more than twenty years and owns her own tour company, Charleston Raconteurs (charlestonraconteurs.com). As Director of Public Programs at Historic Charleston Foundation, Leigh was tapped by the Mayor's Office to serve as coeditor of the city's history and tour guide training manual in 2009. Her first book, *Lost Charleston* (Pavilion), was published in 2019. And in case this writing thing doesn't work out, she is pleased to still have her day job as Chief Advancement Officer at the American College of the Building Arts, where she once had an office in the Charleston District Jail, just down the hall from where Lavinia Fisher awaited her execution.